MW00356186

BEYOND BORDERS

BEYOND BORDERS

Short Stories of a Long Life

ALLAN REDFERN

**Beyond Borders: Short Stories of a
Long Life**

Copyright © 2021 Allan Redfern.
Produced and printed
by Stillwater River Publications.
All rights reserved.
Written and produced in the
United States of America.
This book may not be reproduced
or sold in any form without the
expressed, written permission
of the author and publisher.
Visit our website at
www.StillwaterPress.com
for more information.
First Stillwater River Publications Edition
ISBN: 978-1-955123-00-6
1 2 3 4 5 6 7 8 9 10
Written by Allan Redfern
Cover and book design by Helene Berinsky
Cover photo by Allan Redfern
Published by Stillwater River Publications,
Pawtucket, RI, USA.
*The views and opinions expressed in this
book are solely those of the author
and do not necessarily reflect the
views and opinions of the publisher.*

CONTENTS

AUTHOR'S NOTE

"Nothing like that ever happens to me." That's what some people often say after listening to or reading one of my stories. They seem to think I have a monopoly on the experiences I have had and the people I have encountered. Others may think I just made it all up—not so. However, I do pay attention to what goes on around me. The people I have met along the way have made my journey richer. A quote that I came across from William Lloyd Garrison, American journalist and abolitionist says it all, "My country is the world. My countrymen are all mankind."

Lots of thanks go out to my friends and colleagues for their help in putting these works together. Special recognition to Marita Stapleton for her help with editing and finalizing the manuscript. Also to my dear friend and neighbor Mariann Millette who gave me a big push whenever she thought I needed it—and I needed it a lot. Thank you to Fran and Jim Bedell, traveling companions extraordinaire, and Jane Case, queen of the kingdom known as Blue Moon Farm, for cheering me on. I also recognize Gayle Eaton, Jack Barry, and Susan Berman—all encouraging writers in our writing group in Rhode Island. And last, but not least, my former wife, Susan, whose memory is even better than I thought, which brings up the matter of remembering. This book's contents are only as accurate as my memory allows them to be.

Any misrepresentations are solely my own.

Learning to Fly

I SPEND SOME DAYS SUBSTITUTE TEACHING AT NARRAGANSETT High School. During one such day my last class was a good class, mostly seniors taking Spanish IV. That's one of my favorites. Good kids, and I can usually be a teacher, instead of the babysitter handing out the busy work the absent teacher left for me. Somehow, out of the lesson, we came to talk about Spain, the city of Pamplona, the festival of San Fermin and the annual Running of the Bulls through the streets, in which I have participated a number of times. Kids love that stuff, and so do I.

After some discussion one of the female students asked in sort of a whine "How many countries have you been to anyway?" I said I didn't know but it was quite a few. She said, "You've got a map on the wall right behind you—why don't you count them?" To tell you the truth, I've never much liked the people who counted countries. To me it was like Boy Scouts who collected merit badges for bragging. But I realized we had completed all the work that was left and we had time to spare, so I said "OK."

I turned around and started at the eastern side of the world map and worked my way west to the other edge, naming each country I had visited. When I looked back to the class, one of the kids said "That's 35 countries . . . How old *are* you?"

I was saved by the bell. But it got me thinking about my introduction to travel and my never-ending desire to do more of it.

It was nearly 60 years ago that I learned to fly. It set the course for my life. Most children went to bed and went to sleep. Each evening when I went to bed, before I put out the light, I reached down under my mattress and fastened an alligator clip with a wire to the orderly tangle of exposed bed springs that supported the mattress just below me. Attached to the wire was a Rocket Radio, a simple crystal radio in the shape of a small rocket like a Jules Verne creation. Connected to it was another long thin wire and an ear plug. There was no tuning dial, or volume control. Only a small metal pin like a nose cone on the rocket that you could slide up or down to find a station. It didn't need a battery. All the power it needed came from the transmitter at the radio station. But you did need a good antenna to pick it up—I had my bedspring.

Each evening when things got quiet and dark, I hooked up my rocket radio and my bed became more than a place of rest. It became my magic carpet. The darkness of my room became the night sky as I imagined flying across the earth and connecting with lands and people foreign to me. Early in the night I would find the "easy to reach", less distant stations—the ones in Providence and Boston. And then there was New York—and they were good. Stations like WNEW, WINS, WNBC, WCBS, and WABC. I got to know them all, as I listened in the dark, flying above the earth on my magic carpet. Each contact had a special personality and character that I could recognize before they periodically announced themselves. As the night progressed, I traveled farther west and away, and with the most delicate of adjustments I was able to find KDKA, America's very first commercial radio station, in Pittsburgh, Pennsylvania. I really felt like I was there. Hearing was better than seeing, as I could create my own images of each far-off place and see the people who spoke with the different accents. I could see so clearly from above. Like WLS Chicago, another of my favorite destinations; a big city a thousand miles away. I could see them, but they couldn't see me, or even know of my existence, as I hovered in the darkness above them. And a night wouldn't be complete without a visit to my friends in Wheeling, West Virginia. WWVA with "The All-Night Radio Jamboree." It was music, and laughter, and stories, and went on and on in the most amazing southern accents. They called their station "The Friendly Voice from Out of the Hills." It *was* friendly, and I loved it. I hovered above, listening, usually until sleep finally overcame me.

When I woke with morning light, I discovered everything had been transformed. I lay in my bed, returned from my dreams and the only evidence remaining of my travels was the earplug usually still lodged in my ear.

Gradually, I discovered new places to visit, but I also discovered television, and girls, and a lot of other distractions, including books. One book I read seriously re-energized my travel dreams and when I was old enough, I took action and became a real traveler. My first foreign destination was England, where I stepped from the plane, walked down the metal rolling staircase and bent over to touch the ground to see if it was real. It reminds me now of Neil Armstrong's "one small step for man."

The book that caught me was *The Drifters* by Michener. It's the story of youth and turmoil that drove young individuals away from some things, and toward others. The Drifters met by chance in Torremolinos Spain and traveled around Europe and North Africa and back to Spain and spent some time in—oh yes—the city of Pamplona, the festival of San Fermin and the annual Running of the Bulls through the streets of the city.

And these were my thoughts as I looked around my now empty classroom. They made me think about being called to travel, and the fulfillment of dreams, my dreams, dreams that helped guide the course of my life . . . I sat back for a moment, closed my eyes, and remembered 'learning to fly' in the darkness. . . .WLS Chicago, WNEW New York, KDKA Pittsburgh, and, my favorite, and last stop each night, WWVA, the "Friendly Voice from Out of the Hills," Wheeling, West Virginia.

Crossing Borders

I DRIVE "MEXICO" TO THE BUS STOP. THAT'S HIS NICKNAME. IT sets him apart from others, easy to remember, and of course, not his real name—in case someone important should be looking for him. Everyone down there has got a nickname that says something about them. Another one of my friends is called "Pescuecho" literally meaning "Long Neck." At least that was what he told me, and it did fit well. But this day Mexico sits quietly beside me in the passenger seat. We are early, waiting patiently for the next bus. Sometimes the bus is early and sometimes it's late. Early is the real problem. Once I chased an early bus in my car and practically had to run it off the road to get it to stop and let Mexico board.

He's tired now, almost as tired as I am, but neither of us would ever admit it. We raked leaves all day and bagged them and dumped them all for compost. Mexico and I have been working together, off and on, for about 19 years now. Lots of physical labor for fair wages, and over those 19 years we've gotten to know each other pretty well. He learned more English. . . I learned more Spanish. We both learned what we had to, about each other's cultures and found we are not really so different. We both live in the U.S. Fortunately I was born here. He pays a higher price because he's just an American neighbor. But anyway, he feels lucky too.

We break our silence and chat a bit. I know he crossed the border illegally. To kill time, I ask him what that was like. I wondered what kind of people he met and what he experienced with them on such a dangerous journey. Did they bond? Did they maintain contact in the U.S.? At first, he hesitates, then apprehensively starts to answer my questions. He had almost no contact with any of his marching companions. Almost. Lots of folks have successfully crossed the border

4

and become invisible in the fabric of American life. And they still come, no matter how difficult it is to sneak in, taking a chance, risking their lives, for the opportunities and rewards our country can provide, if they are willing to earn them. . . like Mexico is. He's worked here half his life now. Only twice has he returned to his native Mexico. The last time for a serious family illness. His father was very ill, and not expected to live.

As most immigrants do, he helps when he can, and sends money home frequently by Western Union to help with family expenses like schoolbooks or uniforms, or in this case, family medical expenses. To everyone's surprise, his father made a miraculous recovery and for the second time in his life, Mexico came north, back to the land of milk and honey, the land of good steady work. Each time he crosses the border to go north, he pays dearly...about $6,000. He hires a "coyote" and borrows the money with exorbitant interest which he knows he can pay back quickly from what he earns in the U.S.—as a dish washer, or bus boy, or custodian, or auto mechanic, or farm worker, or snow shoveler, or clam shucker, or fruit picker, or factory worker, or landscaper, or any one of many other jobs, just waiting to be done by these good, honest workers. This $6,000 sum is an impossible feat on Mexican wages. On Mexican wages he wouldn't live long enough to save enough for the trip.

The route changes frequently but he was told it was a one week journey from Last Chance, Arizona on the border, across desert and over mountains, landing in Phoenix, AZ. If they are apprehended by the US Border Patrol, or for some other reason they didn't make it to Phoenix, they would get one more chance for free—but dying makes it a nonrefundable event. This is big, risky, business. . . for everyone involved.

The border crossers are organized into groups, usually of about 20, of various ages, mostly—but not all—male with varying physical abilities. Mexico is strong. He is solidly built with broad shoulders. He was prepared for the difficulties the journey can offer. After all it wasn't his first time. Everyone brings only what they need, and everyone carries their own. The clothes on their back. Food and water in a small backpack. They are told that the route they are taking through Arizona is the safest at that moment. They have to cross mountains, nearly straight up and down, but it has its advantages. The most important, and heaviest thing they carry is water, and in the mountains they can find water to refill their bottles, and therefore they can carry less weight. Before crossing, each is offered a cheap pack they sell for about $40 dollars. It has tortillas, dried fruits and jerky, a few canned goods, a large garbage bag, and of course, bottled water. Mexico, having very little money, worked a deal with two other crossers, equally broke, to share one pack's contents of food between the three, and take turns carrying it. It would be difficult, but for one week they felt they could endure—they had no choice.

It was one night in February of 2015, that this group started walking confidently in the dark. The final count was 17 crossers, four of whom were young teenaged girls, and an unusual three coyotes. Perhaps two were in training. The coyotes demanded attention and obedience as they lead the group. They walked the same trails and carried the same packs, and with their knowledge and experience, would lead them up and over the mountains, across the dessert, through unbearable extreme temperatures, both hot and cold, to Phoenix, their ultimate destination. If anyone fell behind, they would be left behind, and they all knew what that meant.

The coyotes set the pace, and for the first time had a chance to size everyone up. Any group hiking in the wild has its similarities. You have your runners. They are impatient and just want to get there as soon as possible—wherever "there" is. They have the detrimental effect of wearing out others, who try to keep up. That's why the coyotes need to set the pace. You also have the individuals who live every second of the journey and will slow down when given the chance. No matter how slow they are already walking, they can go slower. One way or another, the group can spread out so far that someone can become lost. The only ones who truly know, or at least claim to know where they are going, are the coyotes.

It is difficult walking in the night. But they did a lot of it. Tripping and stumbling, walking into things, or just losing their way temporarily. It happens a lot. The moon may provide some visibility but there are no flashlights or cell phone lights allowed. Seeing can just as easily mean being seen, and apprehension by Border Patrol Agents. They say the glow from a burning cigarette in the crisp night air can be seen as far away as one half mile.

Breaks, called by the coyotes give everyone a chance to rest, and in some cases just catch up. It's a chance to count and the only way they know they still have everyone. The night, especially in the higher altitudes, has one more important feature. But it is a serious enemy. . . the cold. When well-fed, and moving at a moderate pace, it's not so bad, but each night gets colder and colder, and they learn what the garbage bag in the pack is for. It's a big bag with a hole cut in the closed end that one can stick his head through. It becomes sort of a windbreaker. By no stretch of the imagination does this keep them warm. . . but it helps. Mexico's problem, along with the two others sharing the one backpack with provisions they bought was that they had to share that one garbage bag as well, taking turns. Better for them was to keep moving, instead of sitting and shivering violently in the dark on the rocks in the cold Arizona terrain.

In general, darkness is the friend of the crossers. But as the trails taken become better and better known to the border control officers, they apprehend more of the offenders, and swiftly return them to the border, by bus if they are close to "La Frontera." The authorities have technology on their side with night-vision glasses, dogs, four-wheel-drive vehicles, and even helicopters sweeping the land and its known trails. This is a fairly mechanical process, and many crossers are familiar with it, having failed before. The luckiest ones make it all the way. The next luckiest are picked up and returned. The least fortunate are usually discovered by agents seeing vultures flying overhead, zeroing in on dinner.

The newest trails developed by the coyotes do not pass around the mountains but over them. They are difficult to hike, nearly straight up and down, filled with loose stone and ravines. This is where some get hurt. Falls, twisted ankles, broken bones, etc., make it difficult to continue hiking with the group. If someone is unable to go on, others with spare energy and good intent will usually try to help the injured, by supporting them with a free arm, carrying their pack, or even carrying them, hoping for some recovery. It happens—but injuries on the trail usually result in the victim giving up, exhausted and in pain, and they just refuse to get up again. The lucky ones are found, get medical attention, and a free bus ride home or back to the starting gate.

In Mexico's group, one of the men, strong and healthy, about 35 years old, was seriously injured when he slipped, and his leg got caught in some rocks. He fell and somehow damaged his leg muscles. When he finally got his leg free, it was obvious he was in trouble. He limped onward but soon fell to the back of the pack. When someone noticed he was missing, Mexico and one other went back and found him just sitting there, in pain, unable to move. Mexico massaged his leg muscles not knowing what else to do, and got him up and running, so to speak, but even with the help of two, he finally gave up again. He insisted he just needed to rest a bit and would catch up. "No te preocupado" "Don't worry" he said. They gave him some additional water and a tiny bit of food from their meager rations and ran to catch up with the others.

The advantages brought by the trek over the mountains was compromised by the time it took to cross them. Instead of the one-week journey they were promised, it went much slower than expected. Mexico and his two backpack partners anticipated severe hunger with the sharing arrangement they made but were totally unprepared for a ten-day journey. By the time the truth was discovered they had already consumed nearly all the food they had brought. Mexico was starving. They hiked day and night. He shivered in the darkness. He consumed his own body to provide the energy for the walk. He could feel it. Near the end, all he had was water.

But in Phoenix they made their rendezvous and ended up in a van. The van took them north, and east. It was driven by a young man working for the same coyotes, part of the deal already bought and paid for at the border. They dropped the crossers one by one as they crossed the country. They were stopped twice by police and questioned. In both cases they were—for some reason—let go and they continued their journey. "Quien sabe!" "Who knows!"

Mexico got off somewhere in New Jersey where his sister lived. He was tired, he was hungry, but he was safe. He slept like the dead for nearly two days.

Now it was time for him to ask me questions. He has to finish his story. He has more to tell. He asks me if I remember his answer of "almost none" to "did you have any more contact with the other border crossers."

"Yes," I remember.

Well, that first night he slept at his sister's. . . he was awakened. . . by a fantasma. Mexico asks me if I believe in them. "You know. . . ghosts?"

Hmm.

The bus. It's coming. I can see it approaching way down the street. I move to get out of the car, but Mexico reaches over and stops me. He says "Wait. . . answer. . . answer my question."

He asks me again if I believe in fantasmas. I say, "I don't know. . . do you?"

"Yes, of course" he says. "Everyone in Mexico believes in such things. One woke me that first night at my sister's in New Jersey. . . The one from the mountain. That one we had to leave . . . with the bad leg. Remember?"

"Yes," I answer quickly.

"He came to me in the middle of the night. He had to find me. . . to tell me his pain was over. . . he was finally free. . . he finally. . . passed."

Mexico jumps out and quickly raises his arm to the approaching bus. It stops and takes him away

Mudo

M-U-D-O, PRONOUNCED MOO-DOUGH, IN SPANISH, MEANS DEAF. That's the name of the little eight-year-old boy I was introduced to as I first arrived at the ranch house. He was a beanpole, narrow in the shoulders and slim right to the bare feet on the ground. "Mudo y sordo" means deaf and dumb. He is totally deaf and probably doesn't speak because he doesn't know what speech sounds like. What he can do is make sounds, specifically one sound, that goes like this: "AAAAAAAH, AAAAAAH!" He makes it soft, or he really lets it loose, however, and whenever, it strikes him. He became an immediate pain in the neck, pulling on my shirt, or jumping around yelling "AAAAAAH, AAAAAAAH!" He interjected this in every conversation, with everybody, and captured lots of attention but I usually couldn't figure out what point he was trying to make. I quickly felt sorry for him, way out in the middle of nowhere, with no professional help available. What they could do for him back home, with lots of special schooling or maybe even an operation . . . I don't know, but he wasn't getting any of that in the back woods of El Salvador, a true third world country.

He could communicate somewhat. He drew pictures in the air in front of him and emphasized certain points with generous use of "AAAAAAH, AAAAAH!" I was soon to learn that he could communicate, and deaf though he was, he was anything but dumb in the usual sense of the word.

It seemed he was the son of Luis' cousin. She lived elsewhere and the boyfriend and father, a Guatemalteco, was long gone. Mudo was one of two eight-year-old boys under the same roof, both sharing the same sort of history, but with different mothers. It seems like a completely natural phenomenon there, extended families that is, and the practice of being taken in by the relatives.

Mudo was everywhere. Wherever I went, he was there watching me, and commenting "AAAAAAH, AAAAAH!" It could really become annoying, and I would look for opportunities to sneak away, but he was like a fly on flypaper, and the flypaper was me. He started his day quietly about ten inches in front of the cook fire with his dirty t-shirt pulled over his knees and down to the ground, watching the fresh milk heat up, and the beans bubble. This was his quiet time, before he was fully awake. He gathered energy as he crouched there in front of the fire like a snake on a warm rock. Not much later he'd be running around, making noise, being his usual bothersome self. He never missed a thing.

He was fascinated by all and he let you know he was paying attention. If I stared at a rooster, or tried taking a picture of it, five minutes later he'd tug on my shirt holding the very same rooster, struggling to escape, as high to my face as he could reach going "AAAAAAH, AAAAAH!" Sometimes I couldn't see him around, but he would usually just be watching from the shadows somewhere, waiting to pounce.

I spent a lot of time swinging in the hammock, writing in a journal. He would come up to my side and stare at the notebook and watch every letter of every word I wrote down. If I put my notebook down for one reason or another and walked away for a bit, I might come back to find his entry of very well done, "never before seen" characters on 8 or 9 lines of the page. They were like hieroglyphics and really quite orderly.

I couldn't ignore his presence, even when he was quiet, so I started to read to him what I was writing. He poised close and was fascinated by every word, and character, even if he couldn't read or hear a word I was saying. I began to experiment a little bit with him. I drew pictures in the dirt at our feet, and said their names, and drew more pictures. He got right into drawing and soon graduated to the paper and pen I provided. He filled the paper with very creative drawings and began to fill his hands, and feet (he never wore shoes), and legs, and arms with a multitude of pictures until I finally retrieved my pen while he had some free skin left, and I still had some ink. We were surrounded by chickens all day and these were portrayed everywhere, drawn from all angles. . . . wow!

He was a boy of many talents, and a fear of almost nothing. He climbed trees. He caught things—like turtles, menacing-looking lizards half his size, snakes, and once a young crane of some kind that wouldn't stop lunging with its long neck, just dying to pluck out his eyes like grapes. Mudo was a hunter. I tried to get him to not kill the birds in the yard, but he didn't quite get my point, or perhaps didn't agree with it. He went around with his slingshot and he was very good with it. I was finding new little victims underfoot on a daily basis. Once I heard a commotion and I turned in time to see Mudo, astride a galloping horse, hanging on for dear life with his fingers buried in the mane of one very excited, and very surprised-looking animal, just powering down the dirt road by our house.

But oh boy, he could be a real bother. Late at night I would sneak out to find a clearing from which to view the incredible dark clear sky. Just the symphony of insects to accompany the show, at least 'til Mudo found me, breaking the night with a very loud "AAAAAAH, AAAAAH!" He just couldn't help it. . . so much to express, with so limited a vocabulary, to such an inexperienced listener. I put my hand on his head and tousled his hair, like people once did to me when I was his age. I drew his attention in the dark and pointed to one of my favorite constellations directly overhead. Orion The Hunter. It stood out bold and just as clear as a bell. Mudo looked up and wondered what fascinated me.

Bending down low to let his eyes follow my arm, I pointed to the three brilliant stars that make up Orion's belt, and then pointed to three points on my belt to explain what they represent. As usual, he repeated the motions to me so I would know he understood. I next pointed to the myriad of little stars hanging down from Orion's belt, and made motions of a sword, or in the more familiar sense, a machete engaged in back and forth motions like harvesting corn or wheat, or maybe more like a warrior. "Swish, Swish, Swish" He pointed at the sword of stars overhead and energetically "Swished" one, two, three times to show me he understood.

Back in the light of the single light bulb hanging from the tree in the front yard, I brought it all together by drawing the constellation, and filling in as best I could, the full diagram of Orion The Hunter. He was pleased, but I think Orion was only part of it. What really pleased him was the successful communication we had.

He liked to hide things. Things like the keys to the pick-up that were the only keys to the pick-up. It was just a game for him, but people got pretty worked up over it. The whole family looked. I was the one to find the keys, but I have to admit, I cheated a bit because I saw him earlier fussing around the notch of a tree. Although everyone searched, no one ever found the beer I bought and stashed in the back of the family refrigerator. Even threatening motions from Luis' parents with a switch snatched from an overhead tree produced no results except "AAAAAAH, AAAAAH!" I didn't care about the beer so much, so I encouraged everyone to let it pass, and it finally did.

One day Luis and I decided to go on a little excursion to see the nearby town and port of La Union. This was, for some reason, one of those times when getting in the pick-up like the family dog waiting for his master, really worked because we took Mudo along with us. He was a little surprised and was quiet as a mouse just absorbing all the sights of the biggest city he had ever seen. It was obviously a rare event to see so many people and all the activity. And he was a little apprehensive, hiding behind Luis and I, just grasping a hand or a tuck of pant seam. A little while later that day, he had his first glimpse at the ocean and its waves. The immensity and power of the whole thing definitely scared him, and he wouldn't even get close to the Pacific surf. It was silence, and riveted attention, and "hang onto pants legs" for safety—never even getting close enough to touch the water. He finally broke his silence on the way home when I popped out of a gas station with ice cream bars for all of us. "AAAAAAH, AAAAAH!"

As I said, he was a pain in the neck, but at the same time a wonder to behold, as the entire world unfolded for him, piece by piece, to see, and taste, and touch.

I told myself I would leave El Salvador if I sensed my welcome running out, or if I ran out of mosquito repellent, whichever came first. After two weeks I announced my departure, a couple days hence. We had all gotten to know each other pretty well and I felt part of the family. I would miss everyone, and one especially. The night before I left, I took Mudo under the hanging light bulb in the front yard and signed news of my departure early the next morning. I pointed to myself with my thumb, then made a side leap into the next day with an arm movement, and then a motion like a jet taking off in the sky. He repeated the message to me for certainty and clarification several times, and then just fell quiet, sad, looking down at the ground at nothing. Once again, I put my hand on his head, very sad, and then. . . "AAAAAAH, AAAAAH!" He looked up, took me by the hand, and led me to the clearing, in to the sky. He pointed up to Orion The Hunter, and with three little motions picked out the three stars of Orion's belt. Then he pointed three times to where his belt would be. He pointed up to the myriad of little stars of Orion's sword, and pointed to where his machete would be and gave three times a "Swish, Swish, Swish" movement of his arm. He looked up to meet my eye. I looked down to meet his. We both smiled with a knowing, an understanding, a friendship... that would last forever.

Motorcycle Man

It was a hot summer Sunday afternoon and I had a house full of friends. It's amazing how many friends you have when you have a house at the beach and plenty of parking. The beach side of the house with a big deck was jammed with thirty-year-olds with sunglasses, sun tans, consuming copious amounts of cold beer. The music and laughter were rhythmic and loud.

I stepped into the kitchen to check on supplies as another guest arrived. He said "Hey! Something's going on in the street out front, maybe an accident," and then he joined the throngs out back. Curious, I walked out my front door and found it was much quieter on this side of the house. Ten or twelve people were standing in the road, just staring with downward casts and expressions that looked like they should be saying "Oh my God. I can't believe this!" I recognized a couple of neighbors and quietly asked what was going on. My sight was directed to the center of the standees where on the ground lay a man, motionless, his head covered with a helmet. As I approached, I realized things did not look good for the young man. No one even went near him. They stood back with fists curled under chins and whispered to each other. The whole time I'm thinking "somebody should do something about this." But nobody was doing anything about this, and I thought "I'm no doctor but someone has got to try and do something!" I moved forward, knelt and tried to detect breathing through his nose or mouth. A woman standing behind me yelled "Don't touch him! You can kill him if you try to move him! I'm a nurse!" Everyone was silent in the big standing ring around me. They just stared. He wasn't breathing. I reached to find a pulse and perhaps hear a heartbeat through his shirt. Nothing! I looked back up just once, at our nurse, then looked back down and struggled, finally removing his motorcycle helmet.

The crowd grew, but they all just disappeared to me. I don't know what they thought, or did, or even if there was sound. My reality had turned into something different from the people around me, and certainly very different from the hoard of guests a couple hundred feet away on my back deck.

I was a high school teacher and had been offered the opportunity to take a workshop in first aid the previous school year. It was fun. It was informative. It was also free; I was there! We learned the very basics like how to stop bleeding, what to do if someone faints, or chokes in a restaurant. We were told about CPR and shown a little about it but were also cautioned that you have to learn that in a special class. We were strictly entry-level first aid. But, some of it stuck and here I was, about to try my best, with a live audience, for real.

I arched his head a little bit as I tried to remember what they showed us and puckered up. Mouth to mouth with this unconscious stranger, who smelled like beer, gave me a moment's hesitation but that's all. I tried not to think about it and just blew. Nothing. "What am I doing wrong? I can't get air into his chest." 'You may have to clear the airway' I remembered someone saying. I opened his mouth and reached in with two fingers as deeply as I could and pulled out pieces of I don't know what, but it reminded me of the parts you find in the little bag you take out of the chicken before you bake it. I cleared the airway as best I could and got ready to give it another try, not knowing what else to do if this didn't work. But it did work. I inflated his chest! I repeated it, and then began an alternating sequence, pushing down on the heart several times strongly, and then re-inflating his chest. I got the rhythm, and there was no other reality. I was the one laying there receiving help. I was the one in trouble. We were one, helping each other, silently cheering each other on, feeling each other's need to make this work.

Some time went by and I became aware of another person approaching. It was Jeannie, my friend, fellow teacher, and by some strange miracle, fellow classmate in my first aid class. She offered help and I took it. She pumped his chest to move the oxygenated blood; I provided the oxygen to his lungs. There were then three on the team! More time passed and I hazily realized there was something else going on. Help, professional help had arrived. The paramedics knelt over us as we still worked. They checked the vital signs and got ready to take over with real oxygen. "On three. One, two three" . . . .and we were separated. It felt so strange as I tipped back, after kneeling so long in the street, after being one with this man who was now in someone else's care. I was a little dizzy. I saw everyone was staring at me with that "Oh my God" look again, only now there were lots and lots of people that I was seeing for the first time. They wheeled my patient away from me and into the ambulance and I turned around to escape the center. Before, the people could only see my back, and the back of my head. Some stared, some looked at me horrified. My mouth, and chin, and shirt were, I realized, soiled—no, not that word. Let's say they carried a lot of evidence as to what I had been doing. I heard one man dry heave as I escaped the circle. Once outside the circle, which was still abuzz with everyone softly debriefing everyone else, I stopped to take it all in. I was dazed. It was another world, another reality.

And then, I felt a hand on my shoulder. When I turned, I faced my second young man of the day, scruffy, tattooed, with a motorcycle helmet tucked under his arm. He squeezed my shoulder and just said, "Hey . . . . . . thanks man." No thank you could could have been more heartfelt, and sincere. I choked. I couldn't answer. He put his head down and walked away.

I walked away too, back to my house and straight into the bathroom. I pulled off my shirt and tossed it into the bathtub, then washed my face. I could hear the laughter, and the other reality out on the deck. When I stepped out to join my guests, one of them yelled loudly to me "Hey, where the hell have you been!"

Lost and Found

DID YOU EVER GET LOST WHEN YOU WERE A LITTLE KID? I SURE did, and it was frightening. Usually it's over pretty quick because you are quickly found, or you find somebody or a place you know and you move on, but sometimes the memory lasts. . . and it can last you for the rest of your life.

When I was about eight years old my family was living in Providence. My life was pretty normal, I guess. I had one sibling, a sister, much older and going to college in New York City. I remember her not living at home with us and I did look forward to her visits on the holidays, etc.

Somehow it came up that my Big Sister wanted me to come to New York City for a visit. She of course would take care of me and show me around and be really responsible. And I thought it was a great idea too! It didn't happen right away. The idea had to get comfortable, and logistics figured because New York was a lot further away in those days. My sister must have given a heck of a sales presentation because one day I found myself standing on the platform with my mother in Providence waiting for the New York, New Haven, and Hartford Railroad to take me away. Things were apparently a little different back then—you didn't worry so much about things that could go wrong, you had more faith in humanity, etc. I had a ticket, and the conductor, who my mother quickly talked to and thanked in advance for keeping an eye on me, became my temporary guardian. I don't remember anyone thinking this was strange, or that it could lead to lawsuits. Instead, the conductor was really friendly, and all the other passengers around me were really friendly, too! I had a pleasant journey and looked forward to getting to New York City, where my Big Sister was waiting for me to arrive at a place called Grand Central Station.

It was a long ride on the train. I ate my sandwich that my mother had made for me and I looked out the window the whole way. When finally the train plunged into darkness below the city, passengers started fumbling with bags, we slowed down and I knew we were close. It was exciting.

We came to a full stop and I could see out the window that there were millions of people everywhere out there. The conductor said his final good-bye and asked to make sure I was all right. Yes, everything was fine, and I thanked him very much. I stepped off the train to the platform with my cardboard suitcase, into the sea of tall people , . New York City.

Now my instructions were pretty clear—get off the train, and don't move. My sister would find me. So that's what I did. Little by little the crowd cleared, and I could see further without all the tall people, but I couldn't see my Big Sister. I didn't move. I remember looking up at the lights in the cement ceiling. You could see but everything was sort of dark and getting a little lonely as more and more people disappeared. I didn't move . . . but the lights inside the train I came in on went off, and it slowly backed up and out of the station. Now I still didn't move but I was definitely getting a little worried. There I sat on my cardboard suitcase, and it was quiet, and I could see from one end of the platform to the other in the dim light. I was all alone.

What to do? I weighed the choices. Stay there like I was told? Or go find someone to help me? I was afraid to leave there because my Big Sister wouldn't know where to look for me, but I didn't know where to go, and didn't even know where all the others all went. I sat there longer and from somewhere behind me I heard footsteps. I turned and saw three full grown men walking down the platform toward me. I watched them approach in that dim light and could tell that the one in the middle was sort of leading the other two. They got closer and finally came right up to me and stopped. How could my Big Sister do this to me! The leader in the center bent over and put his head directly in front of mine and said "Hello, young man, what are you doing here?" Now another thing I was told about was be careful talking to strangers, but at this point, it was all I had. I gave this total stranger a full account of me and the dilemma I was in—he listened and after a few moments, reached down, took my hand and lead me down the platform, my cardboard suitcase carried by one of the two other men, not looking real happy about it. I was at the mercy of this man and was worried, but he sensed this and stopped to assure me that I shouldn't worry, we were going to find my Big Sister and everything would be all right.

We walked to an escalator and glided up, out of what felt like a poorly lit basement to a magnificent hall with light, and very tall ceilings, and giant windows, and the biggest clock I had ever seen. This is where all the people went! It was loud, and bustling, and I was once again dwarfed by so many tall people—but my friend had me by the hand and led me to a wide stairway in the center of the cavernous hall. Up we walked and came to a door at the top, which my friend opened and when all of us were inside, the door closed, and it was quiet. It was a big office with one big desk, and one woman sitting behind it. She looked up to see who dared enter, and in a moment placed a smile on her face, rounded her desk and came over to welcome my new friend. I was invisible! She excused herself one moment and returned from another door with an older, rounder gentleman introduced as the stationmaster. My friend introduced me and my problem to the both of them. They gave me assurance of help and within minutes I heard my Big Sister's name being broadcast through the terminal, "Please report to the Stationmaster's office immediately!" Wow, I certainly didn't want to cause so much commotion but what could I do?

We waited, and the big people in the room chatted like they were friends, and I sat on a long bench by the wall in front of the huge window overlooking the cavern below us. After some time, they called for my Big Sister again. And still no response. My new friend was getting a little antsy and he finally came over to me and sat down. He put his arm around me and assured me everything would be alright, but he had to leave, and I was in good hands. He said good-bye to all of us and with a smile and a wink, disappeared through that huge office door. I felt alone again. My Big Sister still wasn't there, my friend had left me, and I didn't know what would happen next. The secretary sensed my worry and once again came around her desk and sat next to me. I don't think she had much experience around kids, but she made small talk with me and asked if I knew who my friend was. No, I didn't. She said I should remember how he helped me and told me his name.

Perry Como.

My Big Sister finally gave up looking for me at Penn Station and found me at Grand Central. We had a wonderful time together in New York City, and I had an uneventful train trip home.

I remember getting lost, and I remember being found, and right through the television screen, for many years after, I sent silent thanks to my special friend Perry, who I will remember forever.

Shoeshine Boy

THE SHOESHINE BOY ISN'T A BOY AT ALL. HE IS A FULL-GROWN man who, like all grown men, had once been a boy, but those days were long gone. His work, and his identity, are the same. He is a shoeshine boy—and will be for life.

With a questioning look at the potential customers in the park, he can tell who might be ready to purchase his services. He's searching for leather. Running shoes and sandals have taken so much business away; as had young boys, who should be in school, taking advantage of the opportunity that tourists don't know they are supporting truancy and bad health due to the quantity of sweets purchased and devoured each day. It's hard to ignore the big smiles and cute faces of the children shining shoes. They earn their money, but at the expense of the professionals who have families to support.

Yet there are still many opportunities for the shoeshine boy. Some customers, seeking an image of care, and well-being, and prosperity, actually need a shine, and every day. A shine to remove the effects of a poorly placed step in the otherwise clean, side-walked city of Antigua, Guatemala. I myself take great notice of the irregular pavement and missing cobbles that can cause one to fall or twist an ankle, never mind ruin your shine. Just add the darkness of night, the erratic motorbike, and tuk-tuk traffic all day—they can steal your attention and make it challenging to navigate safely, and cleanly, across a simple street. But need usually has very little to do with getting your shoes shined. Getting a shine satisfies. It improves one's spirits.

But this was not the shoeshine boy's concern. He scans his potential clients for anyone scanning for him. When eye contact is made, there is the smallest of nods to indicate an agreement. A fair trade. A sort of dance. Our shoeshine boy is middle-aged, and he knows the dance well. He approaches with certainty, but not too anxiously. That would look like he was a beggar. And he is not a beggar.

The customer is always sitting. In the park, there are many places to sit—benches are everywhere. Everyone sits, and watches everyone else, a little like a sidewalk café in Paris, but without the café or Paris. The first physical contact between the shoeshine boy and the client is the placement of the customer's foot in the proper position on top of the shoeshine box on a small wooden block meant to firmly catch the heel. The box, made of wood and about the size of a milk crate, is open on one side, and carries all the tools of the trade. It even has its own familiar, unmistakable aroma about it. The shoeshine leans forward on one knee while he stretches his other leg out in front, and balances carefully before his customer. He, like most, also carries a small stool on which to lean his posterior for good leverage. The one knee on the ground might be taken as a sign of respect to a superior, but only to the unknowing, because now, it is the shine boy, who becomes the master.

Out of the box he withdraws what he needs. The tin of polish in the correct color. A glass bottle with a screw top containing some milky-looking liquid, and a soft rag and two brushes—one for shining, one small one for cleaning up the sole and stitches with the milky liquid. This is attention to detail. Some shoe-shines even remove the laces to reach every bit of leather without obstacles. But this takes time, and not all customers are willing to invest quite so much.

The first few moments of the shine are like getting acquainted, but without talking. To start, each pant leg is rolled up a few inches away from any possible contact with the polish. Any obvious, or invisible, specks of soil are rubbed off with the rag and a coarse brush. Occasional taps on the foot mean "switch" and your feet trade places, to put the other one on top of the box. The movements are testing and serve as a reminder of who is in charge. It's another step in the dance. With each moment, more of the heat from the hands of the shoeshine is carried through the leather, made soft now with the softened wax. These warm, busy fingers have long been stained with the colors of the polish. Warm, stained, strong, fingers, doing their dance. Some customers have by this time already closed their eyes, to better feel and accept the touch. Some customers, most often women, remove their shoes and just sit on the bench patiently, avoiding this almost too personal touch. In this case, the shoeshine's hands, one inside the shoe, one out, give and receive all the benefit.

After the polish has been applied the shoeshine uses a clean soft brush to heat it with friction, making the leather even more supple. The brush is passed smoothly, many times around the course of the entire shoe, from one hand to the other without hesitation when it reaches its farthest point at the heel. The pass is smooth and unbroken. After the thorough brushing, the clean soft rag appears and it's the signal, sadly, that the experience will soon come to an end. The customer opens his eyes to the quick back and forth of the cloth and distinctive sharp snaps repeated again and again, and finally it is done. It leaves one feeling pampered and relaxed. One just needs to sit for a few moments to regain a worldly balance...and pay for the shine.

Moments later, our shoeshine is off seeking more good leather.

Ups & Downs

I ONCE MET A MAN IN THE ELEVATOR BUSINESS. HE SAID IT WAS A good job but "It had its ups and downs" and then laughed heartily at his own joke.

But not all of us take elevators so lightly. One of my first jobs, at 16, was at the Outlet Department Store in downtown Providence as an elevator operator. It was fun and I soon got the knack of stopping at just the right level so the floors were even, and nobody tripped. I carefully opened and closed the accordion gate, and I became an expert, answering questions, knowing what things were on which floors—there were six of them, and a basement. "Lots of ups and downs."

I was still there when they went modern and replaced, one by one, all the old elevators with new ones. Just push the button. No more "What floor please?" No more comments on the weather. No more small talk. No more socializing. Some customers were as apprehensive about self-service elevators as some drivers are today about self-driving cars. But I was replaced by elevator music, and everybody got used to it.

They moved me to a position of stock boy for the shoe department. That was good—new things to learn—and I still ran the old freight elevator on occasion.

A couple of years later, I had progressed through the ranks and found myself in the Junior Executive Training Program at the Outlet. I also took business classes as part of the Retail Management program at Rhode Island Junior College, as they called it at the time. As part of my program I was sent to Houston, Texas to compete in business skills against other students from across the country. It was a big deal. The two things from that trip I remember most are lunch with James Cash Penny, and the elevators at the Rice Hotel, where I stayed those four days.

The day before leaving Houston, I got squeezed into an elevator with way too many other students. It was very busy, and no one wanted to wait for the next car. I was shorter than most and being so jammed in, all I could see were necks and shoulders towering above me. I got pushed tighter and tighter to the back of the car. Fortunately, it was a short ride . . . or so I thought.

As we rose, I watched the arrow above the door point to the floor numbers, and then come to an abrupt halt between the sixth and seventh floors. We were laughing, and yelling like it was a big joke, but no matter how many or which buttons were pressed, we did not move. What did work was the red button, the alarm bell, and some-one pressed and pressed again, and finally held it for a long time. This began to look like a real emergency. The bell just rang and rang with no answer.

We weren't laughing anymore. We were jammed tight against each other in sweltering hot Houston, in a box that was way too small for our number. It got hotter. The oxygen got scarcer, and panic started to set in. The yelling became extreme until one guy screamed at the top of his lungs for everybody to just "Shut up! We have to figure what to do." The girl to my front quietly passed out, and melted, but she couldn't even fall—there was just no room. One of the other guys pan-icked and screamed, and squirmed his way up, until he was thrashing and kicking above all the tallest people's heads. Several hands grabbed and held him tight, until his eyes just glassed over and finally closed, perhaps resigning himself to his fate. For once in my life I was glad I was short. This was getting serious. A quiet overcame us.

And what was I thinking? What was I doing? Nothing. I found the whole experience absolutely fascinating. It was like a case study of group dynamics. People fell into roles of followers, or leaders. Some panicked, some rose to the call to figure out how to get us out of this jam. We might as well have been in outer space like Apollo 13. But no one seemed to know we were there, stuck like that. All of us were soaked in our own perspiration, and everyone else's too. The lack of fresh air really began to take its toll. I remember thinking that at least the elevator light worked. This is when someone said "Hey, look up. . . does anyone see what I see?" A small line in the ceiling. Just a crack. We were all spent, and light-headed but this brought new life to our cause. This was an old hotel, painted many times over the years and things like seams of hatches just disappeared. This time we supported the efforts of one guy as he lay on his back, supported by heads and hands from below him as he kicked and kicked the ceiling until a small hatch broke open, and punched right out. A giant flush of cool, fresh air rushed down upon us. We could breathe and we knew we were OK. A couple guys climbed up and out onto the roof of our elevator. That gave us a little room. The girl who fainted was still out but at least she could lay down. The screaming shifted from inside our little elevator car to the elevator shaft, and that finally brought action. People started yelling at us, telling us to stay calm, and help was on the way.

Help was in the form of police, and firemen, and most important, elevator technicians. I wondered to myself if these guys ever told the "ups and downs" joke.

Things didn't happen quickly. Apparently, some serious discussions were going on, but we didn't know how serious at the time. They were afraid of the possibility of the perilously overweight car just plunging seven stories. The first thing that did happen was a free fall of about four feet. We were totally taken by surprise and screamed as the car fell, then stopped and bounced repeatedly. We were now close to the 6th floor.

They decided not to take any more chances and weighed their options. We waited. We heard guys yelling at each other and things banging. Finally, someone yelled at us to back tightly away from the door. We did so and the door sprang open with the aid of wrecking bars and an order to "Stay back-Stay back!" The bottom of our car, maybe 2 feet, was open to the sixth floor. A sheet of heavy plywood was pushed up to meet the floor opening of our car. One by one, as instructed, we sat down at the opening, feet dangling into the corridor. Our rescuers grabbed our ankles, pulled us out and we slid down the sheet of plywood to safety. We were all exhausted. The hour and a half we were stuck seemed much longer. They lined us all up to lay on the carpeted hallway floor with pillows they must have grabbed from rooms. Management was there and gave everyone an ice-cold Coca-Cola in the glass bottle. That's where we were when the Houston Chronicle took our picture. We were all there, 22 of us, except for the girl who fainted. She spent the night in the hospital but turned out OK.

As they say, all's well that ends well. But don't think this experience doesn't cross my mind from time to time . . . like nearly every time I step into an elevator. I've let more than a few overfilled elevators go on without me and I always look up to find the hatch. And sometimes I get a little elevator flashback when I enjoy an ice-cold Coca-Cola . . . especially in the glass bottle.

George

GEORGE WAS A PATIENT. HE WAS ABOUT 70 YEARS OLD AND THE later years of his life were lived in the confines of a State Mental Hospital in Massachusetts. He cruised Upper Hall North, a geriatrics ward, balanced on his one remaining leg, and a crutch. The empty leg of his 'state-owned' stretch pants was rolled up and pinned so it wouldn't get in his way. His face was covered with a heavy silver-gray stubble over an ashen complexion. His head was remarkably full of hair for someone his age, although it looked like a series of cowlicks or better yet, crop circles. His teeth were long since gone and his swollen tongue nearly always protruded awkwardly from the side of his mouth. He spent his waking moments in the pursuit of one thing and one thing only. "Gimme a cigarette will ya?" And that is all I ever heard him say. We would have called him that as a nickname if it hadn't been so long.

George never had a smile, comment, or any communication with other patients or hospital staff that I'm aware of. But through my two-and-a-half years working as Attendant Nurse, as I put myself through college, I heard him say, "Gimme a cigarette will ya?" hundreds, maybe thousands of times. Patients were allowed to smoke when supervised. They weren't allowed matches, but the state did supply the cigarettes which were doled out by us, to patients, for their help. I'm sure this wasn't exactly the intended procedure. But, stripping the beds each morning before the day shift came in was worth a couple of cigarettes right there. The patients capable of handling a broom or mop, were doing the work of the attendants. The cigarettes weren't our cigarettes, they were for the patients. But we attendants had them, so chores were rewarded with cigarettes, and the click of a Bic.

George was a particularly intense smoker. It was difficult to see where his fingers and lips ended and where the cigarette began. He liked to rip off the filter.

I can't say George was a likable fella. You could talk to him all you wanted but got back nothing except his one familiar line. Some of the patients were very likable. There was Elijah for example, an old skinny black man covered with scars. One night he was awake and told me, in a very slow southern drawl, how his daddy would take him out on the Suwanee River in north central Florida where he was raised. He was tied with a rope and cast into the night water for alligator bait. He usually got pulled into the boat before the alligator got hold of him, but not always.

I worked the night shift, 11 to 7, five days a week. I learned a lot. There was "Top fooin round!" another elderly patient. He went around nude all the time, losing his johnny, just hopping around with one gimpy leg. He was another one who didn't converse. . . .and hadn't since he was in the cavalry as a teenager and was kicked in the head by a horse, or so the story goes. The only words I ever heard from his mouth were "top fooin round" and I can't say where they came from. He was best known for taking apart the one sheet he was given, every night. With his teeth and fingers, in the dark, he reduced it to a small mountain of postage-stamp-sized squares. This 'habit' had started long before I worked there.

And there was "Goddamo." He was a big man whose legs hadn't supported him for a long time. He needed to be lifted into a tray chair every morning and into bed every night. "Godammo" was all he said, and he said it a lot. One night he said it again and again and I couldn't understand why. I finally called someone in to look at him. The little oriental doctor who finally showed up in his pajamas with a long coat over them couldn't find anything wrong with him either, but the "Goddamo"'s were coming fast and furious. We left him in bed that morning rather than try to move him. When I came to work the next night, I learned he had been moved to the infirmary with a broken hip. He died two days later.

There were others, some still with stories, and some just existing, disconnected from their former lives. And then there was George.

One quiet night I 'tripped the ward', making sure everything was alright, and then stood in the day room of this old hospital. It had big tall windows covered with heavy screen. The moon was full, and the light poured in, creating shadows and an atmosphere that was down-right spooky. I jumped when I heard out of the darkness, "Gimme a cigarette will ya?" George obviously couldn't sleep and sat in the shadows of the day room. I looked at him without turning on a light. I was tired. I felt like just ushering him back to bed, but instead, in the middle of the night, to his surprise, I presented him with a cigarette, and a light. I said, "Just one George, and what are you doin' here anyway?" It was like talking to a cat. I didn't expect a response but for the second time this evening, I was startled. The moonlight had shifted a little and George was bathed in a silvery spotlight. He spoke. He told me of his life as a troublemaker, a petty criminal, an alcoholic, and finally a skid row bum. He told me how he had cut his foot while living on a sidewalk and lost his leg from the severe infection. He told me of the cold he had to endure, and the dangers of just being homeless. And then he learned somewhere that he could have a home where someone was always there to take care of him. All he needed to do was commit himself and act crazy. He said, "I get three meals, a bed to sleep in, and TV if I want it, and it's always warm in here. And oh yeah, I even get someone to light my cigarettes for me. So, who's crazy?"

George finished his cigarette, and on my suggestion, he cruised back to his bed. After that night, although I sometimes tried to talk to him, even when no one else was around, the only words from his lips forever more were, "Gimme a cigarette will ya?"

Birthday in Havana

MY TWO NEW FRIENDS WERE SITTING ON MY BED AS I EMPTIED my backpack. They were enjoying it, I could tell. Things from the land of plenty. Mostly clothes, but I created a special little pile of official papers. My passport sat on top. Alexi, the one I knew best, but not at all, nonchalantly picked it up and opened it to the front—the part with my picture, name, etc. I pretended I didn't mind. After all they were helping me survive the week. He just stared a moment and then excitedly proclaimed, "Tomorrow is your birthday! We need to have a party!" Carlos got right into it. The two of them finally convinced me. We could do it at Alexi's house where he lived with his mother, girlfriend, and little sister. All we needed was food, rum, and music. The whole barrio would come.

The next morning Alexi and Carlos came to pick me up as promised. First stop was his apartment so I could see what we had to work with. It was a crumbly cement place on a back street in the section known as "Old Havana"—no glass in the windows, no furniture but for a shaky kitchen table and a couple chairs, two small rooms with mattresses, and in the corner, a fridge from the 50's (pre-Castro) with a missing handle. A giant elastic band—a used bicycle inner tube—kept it closed. It was all but empty anyway. The kitchen stove was a propane, one-burner hot plate. I found one dented frying pan, one big spoon, but little else. Alexi's mother in her housedress and apron, stood back. Everyone knew I was in charge of the kitchen for the party. I was having second thoughts.

My second thoughts were about the lack of cooking, serving, and eating equipment we kind of take for granted here. My third thoughts were about the money. I had very little, but I was the "Bank of America" to them. It was my party. I was apparently throwing it for myself, and the entire neighborhood.

Off we went to do the shopping. The only real market in town was the black market. Basic food supplies like oil, and rice, and beans, were bought inexpensively with ration tickets from government stores. The Cubans in 2002 weren't starving to death but seemed close to it. The best food produced in Cuba was exported by the government, for dollars. They needed US dollars for international purchases like gasoline. There really were a lot of good meats, fruits, and vegetables, but they were all beyond the financial reach of the common Cuban citizen.

I spent a lot of time at a meat counter, trying to pick out a piece of beef with fewer flies on it than the others. They had no refrigeration there. This unknown cut of beef determined my menu for the evening: as much fluffy white rice as I could cook, a medley of fresh vegetables like carrots, onions and peppers, with thinly-sliced beef and fresh herbs sautéed in a rich brown sauce with a splash of good Cuban rum, which of course I intended to ignite in the pan with a *woof!* . . . to complete the show.

I started cooking around sunset and the flavors escaped as fragrances. In ones, twos, and threes the entire neighborhood arrived. They needed no invitation. The air was warm. The light was dim, just a single light bulb hanging on a wire. The cement walls were cracked but took on a colorful character. The music was electric—Bob Marley wailing from a boom box hanging from a nail stuck in a crack in the wall. My guests needed drinks! I was directed to a street vendor who sold rum, and just rum, at two dollars for the big one. I could see the crowd was thirsty, so I bought two. The dancing had started. Dinner was served! There was only one plate, but it was filled repeatedly and eaten like finger food as it traveled over heads, around the rooms, and even into the street. Everyone was dancing. They had no glasses. Both bottles of rum were seen again and again, bottoms turning up above heads and shared between all, even the 10- and 11-year-olds. Even Alexi's mother who looked about 75 was getting her share, between puffs on a huge Cuban cigar. I was busy playing host but finally got a little break time after purchasing two more bottles of rum. Alexi's mother, more my speed than most of the guests, and I had a dance, then sat on the two chairs that were, surprisingly, unused all evening. It was then, that Alexi's mother presented me with a birthday present—one of her prized cigars. We sat back together in front of the fridge, hoping the bicycle tube wouldn't pop, and enjoyed our rum, our cigars, the music, and the swell of humanity as it rose and fell late into the night as one with the musical beat . . . a real person-to-person, 'people to people' experience . . . Cuban Style!

Viva la Revolucion! Viva Cuba! Y Feliz Compleaños para mi!

Swiss Family Brager

IT WAS THE SUMMER OF 1971 BEFORE OUR SENIOR YEAR AT UMass. My college roommate Norman and I traveled, or perhaps more accurately, as I look back, bumbled, stumbled, slummed, and slid, around Europe for nine weeks. It was definitely an under-financed excursion, having spent most of our money just getting there and buying student-rail passes. That left me with $165 to spend any way I wanted; I soon realized the 165 bucks was not going to go far. Just getting into the city center from Gatwick bit deeply into our kitty - $11 lost and we hadn't even gone anywhere yet. What were we thinking? We had to be careful, and clever. Eating and sleeping would have to be accomplished in creative ways over that nine weeks, before our return flight snatched us home. It was a rough start and we had to learn how to stretch each of the $10 travelers checks we had tucked inside our backpacks. This was difficult, but it was quite a trip. We got a good glimpse of eleven countries. We spent 16 nights sleeping on trains. We slept under bridges like the homeless. We camped and hosteled, and seemed to get by, although I know I lost 17 pounds somewhere along the way.

We were spending our last full stop before our departure home in a campground, very cheap, in Lisbon. For about a dollar a day we could eat, and sleep, and we were pretty comfortable with fellow hardened travelers sitting around a campfire each evening, sharing stories, as we passed a cheap bottle of Mateus. We stayed there as long as we could to stretch money but then, by my encouragement, we made a mad dash, two days and nights by train to Switzerland, where I had ancestral roots. Time was short but I just had to see it, and Norman was game or maybe just too worn out to protest. Our train left early Friday morning from Lisbon; later that day we crossed into Spain. Sometime Saturday we crossed into France.

We were tired, and hungry, and not very "fresh" what with no bathing, no food to speak of, and the only sleep we had was sitting up between passengers in the compartment with heads bobbing or falling back, mouths open. It's always ugly to watch. It was like a fog, in and out of consciousness with always the steady clickety-clack of the rails, comforting like a "mother's heartbeat." The languages spoken in the compartment switched from Portuguese, to Spanish, and finally to French, and told us of our progress. Oh, and I do remember once waking from the sleep fog to the most beautiful French I have ever heard. An older, very well-dressed woman sat across from me and spoke to her companions on both sides. I didn't understand a word, but it was like music. I closed my eyes to listen all the better. When I next opened them, they were all gone, like a dream, disembarked at some station along the way.

The trains we took were, of course, not first class and not the fastest, and often stopped for no apparent reason, but we made steady progress toward St. Gallen, Switzerland, close to my supposed ancestral village of Appenzell. One thing you learn when traveling on a shoestring, is to avoid Sunday arrivals in a new city. Especially a new city in a new country. Often shops and stores and banks, and the things you need to get settled just aren't open. Before the days of ATMs for example, you needed somewhere to change money.

We arrived at about eight o'clock on Sunday morning after having spent two days and nights dazedly bobbing along. We were feeling pretty worn out, and we looked it too! Our first order of business was to find a place to stay that we could afford. The city of St. Gallen was Sunday quiet. Almost no one was in sight, and when we approached a couple of different people, they veered away from us and spoke only German. Someone finally figured us out, with our poverty-look and backpacks, and pointed uphill and away from the center of town, "JUGENHAUSE!" OK, we had a direction to move in, and the German word for "youth hostel." In case we got lost, we could use it again. It was slow going and the two days without good food, just sitting on trains, had taken its toll. It took until mid-morning to arrive at the door of a beautiful hostel overlooking the entire city below, only to be told that we couldn't come in—closed until three o'clock in the afternoon by house rules. We had five hours to wait.

We turned and walked aimlessly downhill until we found a quiet bench by a tram stop and sat down. It was almost like we were back on the train but a little hungrier, a little more tired, and oh yes, it started to rain. We didn't care, we were zombies by this time and three o'clock would eventually come. A few people walked by us, glancing and wondering I'm sure, if they should call the police or something. They all had umbrellas. We just got wet. One apparent family—mother, teenage daughter and son walked by and gave us the same stare of wonderment as the others. About an hour later, this same family walked back up and past us again, giving us the same stare. We just got wetter, but we didn't care. We slipped back into our zombie state.

A short time later I became aware of a young man, standing in front of us speaking loudly, trying to get our attention in what I'm sure was very good German but it was like Greek to me. Norman and I looked at each other and wondered if we should do something, or perhaps he was telling us to go away . . . we didn't know. He abruptly stopped talking, frustrated, and quickly reached for my bag and started running up the hill. This brought us to life! We yelled "HEY!" and, not wanting to leave our only possessions, picked them up and scrambled up the hill after him. He probably hadn't been riding on a train for two days because he was pretty spry, and we couldn't catch him. We kept him in sight, and he knew it. He ran through the door of a three-story house and so did we, hot on his heels. He ran up a tall stairway. We dropped our bags and ran up after him, yelling all the way. When we got to the top of the stairs, there was only one door, and our thief had already slipped inside. I reached up to start pounding on the door but it swung open wide, and standing there, out of breath, was our thief. Next to him were the mother and sister of the family we had foggily registered as having walked by us, twice, as we sat on the bench looking hopeless in the rain. Smiles, and repeating one word I can still hear, "wilkommen, wilkommen", they stood back, motioning us to enter, welcoming us into their home.

This was the start of three wonderful days. We became not only human, we were treated like royalty, and then family. We stayed with them, ate with them, laughed with them, and cooked and cleaned with them. They spoke no English and we spoke no German. We got along famously.

Years later we all sat on my porch in Rhode Island, after a big dinner. I had visited them numerous times over the previous thirty years, as they had visited me. We spoke as we sat with our now extended families, of that very first Sunday in Switzerland, in the rain. It was a moment of reflection and it became important to me to express what their kindness on that day had meant to me. I told them how it had in fact changed my life. I hadn't been the same since and always looked for opportunities to pass on a "Willkommen" welcome to others as they had "taught" me. A little shocked, they all looked at me blankly, and stared a moment before anyone spoke. Our thief, much older and no longer a thief, spoke clearly in German on behalf of he and his family. It was they who needed to express thanks and have thought so all these years. They were very brave to have welcomed us that day in Switzerland. It was not like anything they had done before, but because of that wonderful experience, had done so many times since and this had changed their lives.

Moroccan Holiday

It was the summer of 1971. I was attending the University of Massachusetts at Amherst and had one more semester to complete my bachelor's in education. My two housemates were also Ed. Majors. Pasco, anxious to get a job, registered for classes and finished that summer. Norman, after quite a bit of coaxing, came with me, to Europe for nine weeks of touring bits and pieces of 11 countries.

Norman and I learned pretty quickly how to husband our meager resources. One trick was to treat the long-distance trains like hotel rooms. We'd often board a train late in the day, for who knew where, switched trains halfway through the night, and got off again where we started. This saved a lot of money. Hotel rooms and hostels were for shaving, and showering on occasion, when we really needed it. Nonetheless we were having a great time—visiting lots of sights brimming with history, meeting lots of interesting people from all over the world and exchanging travel tips with those we encountered. One guy, an Aussie if I recall, told us about his favorite stop...Morocco. It sounded exciting, and it seemed both do-able and affordable, a short ferry ride across the strait of Gibraltar on the south side of Spain.

Why not? It wasn't planned in any way, but neither was anything else we were doing. We had already intended to go to Spain. Just a short, exciting, little side trip to another continent . . . Africa! Maybe even a little trip on the Marrakesh express, the title of the song that Crosby, Stills, Nash and Young made famous. At this point we couldn't get the music out of our heads.

Two weeks later we were on the edge of the continent. We took the ferry across the straits to Tangier. Late at night we arrived. We didn't know where we were headed but we walked to land from the pier and were met with humanity, in great numbers. Mostly men, in various types of clothing. Most with covered heads. There and then we learned our first words of Arabic—"Backsheesh, backsheesh!" "Gift. . . gift". Or "Help me!" Beggars! The crowd enveloped us, and we struggled out of their grasp, and hurried inland to the exit from the port. But we didn't know where to go. We needed a cheap place to stay, and a bite to eat. We took a chance on one young man who hailed us repeatedly, "Mister mister!" We told him what we needed, and he said he had a "cousin. . . good place to stay. . . very cheap! Two minutes' walk ...follow him please mister ...no problem." He tried to help us carry our packs but we put him off. He led us up a sleeping street, very dark, no one to be seen, and then a man yelled a question in English to us from out of the darkness.

"Where are you going?"

I answered. "We are following this man to a place we can stay tonight."

I heard him spit. And then he answered: "You are following this man to the place where you will be robbed tonight."

The two Moroccan men started yelling at each other. I don't know what they said, but we ran back down the street we had come from, back toward the pier. There we spotted what looked to be a small guest house and we banged on the door until it was answered by a middle-aged man who spoke English...but with a German accent. The windows were all barred, and the door looked more appropriate for a prison than a guesthouse. I didn't know if they meant to keep people out, or in. He put us up and we paid with all the Spanish pesetas we had. Any port in a storm, and this was like a nor'easter. "Let's get the hell out of here as soon as we can!"

The next morning was clear and sunny. There were people in the streets. Everyone seemed a bit friendlier. We may have just gotten off to a bad start. There were still beggars, but they were more interested in the wealthier-looking tourists. We watched and noticed the most successful beggars had the most serious afflictions. We saw one mother with an infant in her arms twist her child's arm every which way as the baby screamed and cried. Someone explained to us it was quite common. It was to help the little boy beg when he got older.

We went back to our little hotel and took advantage of the shower (as long as we had already paid for it). We felt like new. We left our bags and took another short walk to a street restaurant that served egg sandwiches...they were cheap and hit the spot. Business was slow so the man who ran the food stand got talking to us. We didn't know it but there was a lot going on. First and foremost, we had just missed a coup. A couple days earlier some members of the military attempted to assassinate King Hassan II, King of Morocco. In the morning light, we could see pictures of the King everywhere, in every storefront, on the sides of buildings, and there were even small King parades of loyalists marching down the street with posters on sticks. Everyone demonstrated loyalty—the alternative was not favorable. The coup had failed.

When we looked up, all the tall buildings had groups of soldiers taking turns aiming at everybody in the street with machine guns. This was big. It was a good thing we were leaving town, back to Spain, as soon as we could get a ticket out.

Then our guy told us about another little problem. It seems there was a serious typhoid epidemic going on. And you could get into Morocco, but you couldn't get out. The only way you could re-enter Spain for example, was to show proof of vaccination. But the good news was that shots were free, right in the street. They had established stations with health care professionals, if you could call them that, to administer what we needed to get out of the country.

We went back to the hotel and grabbed our packs, and off we went looking for our free shots. We had to hurry. There was a ferry leaving shortly so if we were lucky, we could get shot and still make it to the ferry on time. But "Ohhh!" we thought when we saw it—the line of shot seekers stretched halfway down the block. We joined it and crept ever so slowly toward freedom. The street clinic consisted of a man who wore a dirty lab coat that used to be white, and a nurse assistant, with a sour puss. Nobody talked. Especially as you got nearer to the hypodermic needle. They had set up a table with a grungy tablecloth, and a gas camping stove with an aluminum saucepan half-filled with boiling water. The procedure was: bare your arm, the doctor attached a needle from the tabletop to an oversized hypodermic plunger (like for horses), and he squirted a little vaccine into your arm. He eyeballed the quantity. The needle came off. And it was tossed into the saucepan on the stove, simmering, getting clean for other patients. Again, a needle is picked from the tablecloth and attached to the plunger, and another little squirt into the next patient...all day long. When I was next in line, I found it wasn't as bad as it looked. I was lucky. Norman on the other hand looked the other way and surprisingly yelled. It's hard to believe, but they used the needles so many times they had become dull. The nurse plucked out the needle that was stuck in Norman's arm, and held it up for all to see. It was bent in half—like the letter L. Her sour puss turned into a crude laugh. The doctor didn't say anything. He just looked like someone who needed another drink.

They signed our proof of vaccination papers and we ran like hell to the ferry landing. Almost home! At the gangway they asked to see our proof of vaccination... and then stopped us in our tracks. We had each received a shot just minutes earlier but, they explained, to be effective, it takes two shots, with a minimum of seven days between them.

Apparently, we were trapped like rats, in Morocco, in a typhoid epidemic, with machine gunners on the roofs, mothers breaking young children's arms, would-be robbers, and not many dirhams in our pockets to rob. Who could know how much excitement was coming our way for at least another six days? But Tangier was seedy, and there was no denying, we felt unsafe. We could feel it in the air, so it was off to the train station to check our options.

We bought tickets for the night train to Marrakesh, once again, saving the cost of a hotel. Not a lot of passengers that night on the Marrakesh Express. And no one was singing. We stretched out as best we could on third-class, hard wooden benches and woke in Casablanca at dawn. And it was white, blanca, as the name suggested. Short buildings nestled among the taller, more modern ones, but all were white. They reflected the sun, and avoided much of the heat, which was beginning to be more noticeable, and uncomfortable. We progressed south, to Marrakesh, the gateway to the Sahara Desert—and the inspiration of a damn good song, underappreciated in Morocco.

By mid-morning we had arrived and found our way to the central square, the colorful historical center of the city. It was early and it was quiet. The populace was still waking up, but the square filled steadily as they came out of the desert, drawing with them their camels and beautifully wrapped bundles of items they hoped to sell that day. Whole families, including the smallest little tykes, with big wondering eyes staring at us, arrived in the square.

Norman and I got lucky and found a cheap and safe room in a two-story building, with an open window that faced the square. Just a mattress on the floor. No sheets. No shower. No running water. No screen in the window, or glass. A shared toilet was down the hall. Home sweet home. We were glad to get it.

We stowed our packs and went in search of food. There were several options, but we didn't recognize what they were or know how much they cost. The closest to recognizable were oversized donuts. They were fried before our eyes in what looked like old crankcase oil and then sprinkled with sugar. Tasty. As for the price, we'll never know because we just held out our hands with coins and they took what they needed (or wanted). But it was cheap.

Things began to liven up. Over the course of the day we saw storytellers with rapt audiences, jugglers, snake charmers, musicians, magicians, dancers, acrobats, and lots of vendors selling things we sometimes couldn't even identify. But it was the storytellers, I believe, who were most popular. Many individuals, mostly men, sat quietly on the ground and listened carefully, intently. The well-practiced storytellers held their audience in the palms of their hands—and though maybe only the smallest of the small coins made it into the basket that passed among the audience, most listeners left them something. (Baksheesh and well deserved!)

When the sun left the sky and fell below the desert horizon, the atmosphere changed again to be more and more mystical. The only light came from torches and lanterns. We were tired and wanted to take advantage of that mattress on the floor, but we needed to eat a little something before crashing. We had our eyes on a food vendor selling something like a shish kebab. Small pieces of meat skewered and cooked over charcoal, eaten with a piece of unleavened bread. We were hungry, and it looked mouth-watering. We each bought one and learned later it was camel liver, considered a delicacy, and our hunger made it even better,

I stepped back, out of the torch light and took it all in. The whole scene. What a foreign country this was! As I watched, a group of three young women, appeared out of the darkness. One was nursing a baby and I watched. This was their way of life. But then I heard the young mother plead "Baksheesh. Baksheesh" to Norman. He didn't hear her. But I did. She then reached over to get his attention, lightly touching his arm. So common was this from the beggars that they were often just swatted away, not even deserving of a glance. I saw Norman do this very thing in the torch light—taking one of his hands off the sandwich he was struggling to eat. A small piece of meat tumbled from his grasp and fell to the ground in front of her, but to Norman it meant nothing. He was totally unaware of what had happened. The girl came to attention and her eyes darted from person to person, from side to side. Her eyes locked on to mine, she knew I saw, and I stared back—a brief moment. She snapped to the ground, grabbed the morsel, popped it in her mouth and ran into the darkness of night as if in fear for her own life, and her baby's.

Another incident occurred shortly afterwards. Walking back to our room we came upon a man in an alley yelling at a young boy and beating him unmercifully. Norman and I looked at each other and had the urge to try to save the boy but a man on the other side of the action saw us and raised his hand to get our attention. His index finger waved side to side to us and we knew it was a warning to not interfere for our own good. We took his advice and went back to our room, and just crashed.

We left Marrakesh the next morning. In case anybody is counting, that's four days. Three to go, to get the hell out of Morocco.

So far it looked like neither Norman nor I had contracted typhoid since we had been there. And it didn't seem like the soldiers were aiming their guns particularly at us, but we still had to be careful.

The most fortunate part of the train ride back north was the coastline we observed. I was hanging out the window and yelled to Norman, "Hey, look at this!" It was a campground on a beach. A sign in English identified it as Asilah. I wrote it down. It was less than an hour or so from Tangier. We had three days left in Morocco. We needed a cheap, safe place to stay. When we arrived at Tangier, we turned around and back we went on the next train to Asilah.

Asilah was a nice respite. Camping on the beach was cheap. The town was small but pleasant. If there was a negative, it was that the military defending the King was following us all the way. More machine guns on the roof tops.

We had thin, light sleeping bags - part of our packs. In Germany we had purchased a lightweight two-person pup tent for $16, and a very small "camping gas" stove. We were golden. Up the slopes from the beach was the town. A hotel, a small grocery store, and a cantina. What else do you need? Safety. And it came with the camp site: a teenaged boy security guard walked around between the tents, all night, carrying what looked like a baseball bat to fend off would be robbers. During the day, we relaxed on the beach, walked around the town and shopped for food at the store. The cantina looked like fun if you had even a little extra money. It was full all day and nearly everyone in the town was either inside, or as close as they could get, even jammed into the empty windowsills of the adobe building.

We found out why. They were all fixated to a black and white television set that was propped up high on a table so as many as possible could see. It was a live broadcast. The trials of the individuals who failed in the attempted coup. You needed French or Arabic to fully understand, but we got the gist of it. Each of the accused was given his five minutes or so to state his case, and then the gavel came down. It looked pointless, a mere formality. Each night, the convicted, and they were all convicted, were marched to a long cement wall, with hoods over their heads, and stumbling in chains. A firing squad, on signal, just shot them all dead. Each day was the same. Nearly 500 over the course of the week. It made quite an impression on the populace, including Norman and me. You could understand the loyalty parades. They were nonstop, even in the little town of Asilah with its one television set.

I had a fitful sleep that night. We needed to leave Morocco. We were close.

Very tired, I dozed off on the warm, beautiful beach that next day and was awoken by a strange sound and a camel's face just inches in front of mine. We both startled and jumped, and I safely rolled out from under him. His master, walking toward us from down the beach, thought this was very funny.

It was just one more thing.

Finally, day seven came and we caught the train back to Tangier. We found our vaccination station. Right where we left it. The doctor still in his grungy lab coat. The nurse with her sour puss, but this time, no bent needles. We made it on the ferry. And we were off, off to find our next adventure, unless one found us first.

My Friend Norman

MY FRIEND NORMAN HAS BEEN A FRIEND SINCE COLLEGE. WE were classmates and then roommates, and then friends for life, at least so far. We have endured and assisted each other in deaths, and marriages, and divorces, and other life stuff.

When I meet new people, sooner or later, Norman stories come up. Quite frankly the human side of all of us allows us to recognize a bit of ourselves in Norman.

Like, I remember when Norman graduated from UMASS and found himself a new job and a new place to live. It was a rooming house in East Hampton, Massachusetts, right across from the Kellogg Brush Company, the area's largest employer. The house itself was two stories: a living room, a kitchen/dining room, two bathrooms, and five small bedrooms, three up, two down, fully occupied by men of different ages who all worked across the street in the brush factory—except for Norman. He was the new manager of a small convenience store downtown. It wasn't going to be a career, but it was going to keep him going until the right job came along. None of the four other boarders in this house had come close to his achievement or was likely to in this life.

Now Norman, who for the past several years lived in that unreal, artificial environment called college, was well aware that this was different than he was used to, and that he didn't quite fit in. He didn't have any tattoos, and still doesn't as far as I know. He was groomed, though his blond hair was a little shorter than that of his new housemates, and he dressed clean and casual like a store manager on his day off. He walked in with books under one arm, and in the other, held high, a wire coat hanger with several ties dangling loosely just above the floor as he cut through the middle of the living room. His new housemates eyed him with suspicion and gave each other looks like "Who is this guy? What is he doing here?" and "Who does this college boy think he is? How many ties does he need?" Perhaps they felt that Norman thought he was superior. It was an awkward start to be sure. To top it all off, he moved in on a Sunday, so all the guys were there, in the living room, sitting on slightly beat up overstuffed furniture, watching sports together, drinking beer. No one offered to help him. No one jumped up to shake hands. They sat in their individual chairs like they owned them, and maybe they did. The introduction was less than warm. To make matters worse Norman blocked the TV screen every time he carried a load through the living room to get to the stairs. He could only wonder what they said about him each time he walked back out, through the screen door and out to his car. Well, he was going to have to prove himself, but that was okay, he was a good regular guy, and they'd figure it out.

After Norman got all his stuff upstairs, he figured he'd get his room arranged a bit before venturing downstairs again. He quietly pulled the door of his room closed until it clicked, and then went to work. He hung his clothes, filled the bureau and put boxes under the bed that just didn't fit anywhere else. And then, it was time to go downstairs and get to know his new housemates . . . and hopefully make a favorable impression on them, as just one of the guys.

He tried to turn the door handle, but it seemed stuck. It wasn't stuck. It was locked, as it did automatically each time it was pulled closed. That's what the click was. He was given two keys. One for the front door, and one for his room, which he then needed to unlock it. Norman had the keys. Well, at least remembered where they were. They were dangling from his car ignition.

Now this was embarrassing. He realized that the first real contact he was about to have with his new housemates was him yelling loudly for help, from upstairs, through a locked door. The college boy, on his first day there, had locked himself, in his own room and couldn't get out. Jesus!

Norman tried again to force it, but it was a good lock, and a strong door. He finally just sat on the bed, trying to think of a less embarrassing solution. That's when he went to the window to see if there was another way out. He was on the second floor, and there was nothing in the yard below him, and it just didn't look so very high up. He imagined climbing out and lowering himself down to his fingertips. From there, it certainly wasn't that far down. It would be a gentle drop to the soft-looking lawn under his window. Norman wasn't particularly athletic, but this didn't look that bad. He only wondered whether they would notice when he came in the front door again, without having come down the stairs. He might have to admit the mishap. They could all have a laugh over it. Sort of an ice breaker. And anything was better than yelling for help. How embarrassing!

So he popped the window screen but it slipped out of his hands and bounced off the side of the house. Oops! He quietly waited. Nothing. The TV still blared... no one had noticed. He climbed out, one leg after the other until he sat on the sill, facing outward. Then he turned, committed, and locked his fingers over the bottom of the window frame. He stretched down as far as he could reach, and just hung there for a moment—a moment that included looking down and thinking "Holy Shit!" as he realized that this was a lot higher than he thought. In a panic he tried to pull himself back up, but slipped, and went tumbling down, right past the window by the television in the living room, where sat all his new house mates. To say they were startled to see Norman fly by on his way down is an understatement.

Norman was conscious but hurt, unable to move. All his housemates ran out and found him sprawled, in pain, with one obviously broken leg. They stared, open-mouthed, in disbelief, before someone ran into the house and called the rescue squad for help. Norman's last glimpse of his roommates that day, was the one he remembers still as they stared at him in awe, just before they closed the ambulance door. He certainly knew how to make an impression.

Norman recovered with time. His roommates came to accept him as one of the guys, a regular good guy. They even arranged to trade his room for one downstairs to make it easier for him with his cast and crutches. And the first floor would be a little safer.

Moving Professionals

I USED TO GET BORED. I WAS A TEACHER AND IT SEEMED LIKE every 10 minutes or so, we were going off on another school vacation. It sounded pretty good, but in reality, I needed something to keep me busy. Something new and fun, and something that would enlarge my world. That's when I heard a commercial for an agency. A temporary employment agency. It sounded right up my alley. Walk in, sign up, and join the underemployed.

I was there at 6 o'clock in the morning waiting for my first assignment. It felt a little like a waiting room at the hospital. A variety of people with different skills, and different looks to go with them. I knew they could all tell I was a newbie. I sat close to the edge of my chair just waiting to jump up for some dream job. And then it happened. A manager of sorts called me over to his desk to ask me a couple of questions. "Was I strong? Did I have back problems? Would I be willing to work with a mover for the day? You know, a professional outfit like those with the big ad in the Yellow Pages." Not what I expected, but it was my first opportunity and I didn't wanna blow it. They told me where to go to meet up with the people I'd be working with. There were two, burly-looking, "moving company professionals". And then add me, a schoolteacher, more interested in the experience than the money, sitting right up there between them in the huge tractor trailer.

We headed to East Greenwich, a very nice old-money neighborhood. The home was beautiful. The homeowner, a middle-aged professional of something or other, maybe an attorney, had waited for us, to show us around and answer any questions we might have had. He was also sizing us up. At least two of us looked like they had done this before. He then left us to our task. I didn't know what to do but my two coworkers didn't hesitate to tell me. "Empty the whole goddamn house, piece by piece, until the truck is full, or the house is empty, whichever comes first."

One guy stayed in the truck and packed everything tight; the other guy crammed small items in cardboard boxes with other small items. He told me they used lots of boxes 'cause they charged extra for every one of them. And the third guy, me, just kept lugging everything out of the house, to the trailer's tail gate. There was no slack time—once we got a rhythm, we were all business. These people had some pretty nice stuff. Including an unbelievably heavy grand piano. We took the legs off it and tipped it on its side and voila! On wheels and up to the lift gate it went. I learned a lot of tricks of the trade. When something was too tall, instead of saying "It's too tall...watch it!", I learned to say "Robert Hall." This was trade lingo and it referred to a discount clothing store that advertised heavily on television in the last century. They achieved low prices with "Low overhead."

By early afternoon we were nearly done. Each item I carried out was carefully placed to use every inch of space, top to bottom, side to side, and front to rear. An item that gave the packer in the truck the biggest problem was a very old-looking spindle chair. He tried all positions, twisted and turned and then told me to take it back... he'd get it later. He asked for it again sometime later when he thought he could fit it in... but again passed it back down a failure . . . it was an awkward piece . . . even I could see that. We were getting to the end. We were all tired. I ached. He looked down and said, "let's have that f-ing spindle chair again." I passed it up and he tried every which way, but it was a "no go." He was more frustrated and getting mad. When he turned his face to mine it was red. He said, "get out of the way." I stepped back and he raised the spindle-back chair over his head and threw it straight down to the pavement next to me... and there was nothing left to load but pieces. I just couldn't believe it. He said, "It'll fit now. . . pass it up." This moving business was getting to be pretty exciting. It got even more exciting when the homeowner dropped by to see how we were doing. "Oh. . . things were great. No problem. . .

almost done." The homeowner then asked if we had packed that little spindle-back chair yet—it had been on his mind. He said it was a valuable heirloom and he wanted to take it in his car, just to be safe.

"Oh . . . heh . . . it's packed way up near the front. We can't get it out now. But not to worry, it's safe and sound. We are moving professionals." I was practically choking on my silence. The chair lover then said he would feel so much better if he could have it now. The moving professional said it would add a day to the cost of the move to unpack, and pack all over again. "Well OK . . . if you're sure . . . it's safe" "Yeah...no problem."

Someone eventually was going to have to "face the music" on that one. . . I knew it wouldn't be me. I was a temp.

I was dead tired and sore as we rode back to the terminal. These guys were leaving for the drive to California, early in the morning. I was glad I wasn't going with them, these "moving professionals," I needed to take the rest of the school vacation week off and hope for a speedy recovery.

Looking at Myself

You know what they say, "It's tough getting old. . . but it sure beats the alternative." Really? I sometimes wonder about that. I'm pretty sure there are some examples we could all cite that would have ended better with someone "going gently, into that good night."

I remember my father and his aging. He had no serious health issues as he rose into his eighties. At least not on the outside. What he did have was dementia. It started with little things like driving but forgetting momentarily where he was driving to. Sometimes he would wonder where the milk was and find it in the cupboard next to the canned beans.

He would also believe someone had regularly broken into his house and stolen some item or other that had gone missing. I spent a lot of time debunking this, but to no avail. He lived alone in the house I grew up in. My mother had passed away quietly in her sleep some years earlier. It was just him, and me, wondering what I could do to help him. I tried to organize his surroundings to make it less difficult for him to be confused. I visited him frequently and challenged him, to keep his mind active. The Visiting Nurse service stopped by once a week to make sure he was on course with minor meds and eating properly. But he was slipping. Then, I tried taking him home with me, but he was lost in unfamiliar surroundings and would wake up in the middle of the night yelling for help because he didn't know where he was. Finally, at work, I received a call from the police saying he was found wandering lost around the neighborhood. He could no longer live alone. I couldn't give him the care he needed in my home. So, I started shopping, shopping for the option that was the last thing I wanted to do for him, because I knew it would be the last thing I would want for myself.

I checked out nursing homes. He had some money, but I was amazed how quickly money could disappear in such a place. I immediately crossed off my list any places with fancy chandeliers, and dress codes for dinner. That was not his style. His needs where minimal, really. He needed room and board, and someone to talk to for company—and amusement—and help when he needed something else. I finally found the right place. It was homey. It was close. It provided the care he needed without going overboard. And it was affordable, and we had the funds enough for at least a couple years. When I introduced him to his new home and housemates, they hit it right off. Before I finally left him that day, he had taken his clarinet out of its case and had everyone singing along like they were young again. The home director, sensing my apprehension comforted me as I left that day with the words, "Don't worry! Everyone loves your dad. He's going to be fine here." And he was fine, but dementia is a slippery slope.

I visited him a couple times a week, and usually found him in sort of a day room, or dining room, with all the other residents. I would spot him and say something like "Hey Dad, how's it goin'?" He would glance up at me, and focus for a second, and give me a standard acceptable answer. He was OK, but little by little it showed that he was slowing down and was less alert. He didn't converse much with me, or others. He ate, and slept, and fell deeper inside himself. The clarinet was no longer an option. The Director asked me to take it home with me where it would be safer. He just lived, and I had to be content that we were still "beating the alternative."

One day I stopped in at lunch time and found him sitting at a small square table with two other residents. There was an empty place, an empty chair. I sat down. But, unlike before, I did not speak. No one spoke to me, or even seemed to notice me. I just sat and watched. The other two gentlemen were served plates of a homey comfort food like meatloaf, canned peas, mashed potatoes and gravy and my father perked up enough to ask "Hey, where's MY food?" The aide said, "You already ate!" He couldn't remember. He sat back, quietly resigned. I felt the need to break the silence between us. I started to talk at the table in general about nothing. . . about the weather. . . the news. . . the. . . it didn't matter. It was like talking to the furniture. And when I stopped midstream, no one noticed. This was the first time I hadn't introduced myself to my Dad with a big "Hey Dad!" and a hug. It suddenly occurred to me that he didn't know me as I sat there with him, and maybe without my normal introductions, would not have known me, for a while. I sat quietly and realized we had reached a new level—not of familiarity, or closeness—but remoteness. I just stared, taking in the reality of this.

I spoke cordially with a young woman who came back to the table, to clear the dinner plates and when I turned back to my father, his face was contorted in a strange way. He looked terrified! His eyes locked to mine, and I felt them drill deep into my soul. He then spoke loudly and clearly, to everyone, and no one, "I feel like I'm looking at myself!" I froze with the meaning. Then he slowly withdrew, slipped back, eyes vacant, to deep within himself. I reached over the table and covered his hands with mine, but felt no return, no response. He was gone. . . I had missed him.

It was just two years that he was there. He didn't die right away. His mind was gone, but it failed to convey this information to his body. He was found dead on the floor next to the "bed with the safety railings" that he had successfully climbed over. He left me finally, for that "gentle good night" . . . and left me wondering, if perhaps, as he was looking, and recognizing himself in me, if I wasn't looking, and recognizing myself. . . in him, in good time.

The Bridge

I WAS OUT LATE, AFTER A LONG DAY, JUST WANTING TO GET ONE last thing done. I had set up sort of a dress rehearsal, a walk through of the WaterFire Sharon, PA wood boats with full crews, just like it would be at the first fire coming up in two weeks. It was almost midnight; the city streets were empty. The Shenango river stretched below, moving slow and easy as it worked its way south. We were all tired, but the only thing I cared about now was timing the three boats as they went through their paces of a procession; picking up the flame and cruising past all the braziers just as they would on the night of the first fire. I figured the whole process should be a smooth 18 minutes if we got it right.

We had come a long way. Two years talking, planning, and building. Learning, training and explaining what WaterFire is, and isn't. We were coming down to the wire and we were as good as we were gonna be. I've been volunteering for WaterFire for 20 years. It's an art installation created by Barnaby Evans in Providence, RI that combines floating iron braziers filled with burning wood, with volunteers in special boats keeping those braziers lit while music from around the world fills the air. I was here in this small town in western Pennsylvania to bring WaterFire to life as they used it to bring their down-on-its-luck, rust-belt town back to life.

I stood high above the river on the sidewalk at a midpoint between the 55 braziers. I could see the boats, but they wouldn't see me, and I didn't want them to. They had to watch themselves, just as we had practiced. I was very proud of them.

It was then that I noticed approaching in the darkness, a ways down the sidewalk, a small group of young men. I was watching the boats as they silently went through their maneuvers but as these young men approached, I noticed them sizing me up and I sensed danger. Yes, the body language, the stares, the facial movements betraying the otherwise quiet talk among them, as they approached closer. I had thoughts of quickly stuffing my money in my sock, or in my hat, but it was too late. They kept walking straight at me. Our eyes locked together. They were three rebellious looking, 16- or 17-year-olds. They displayed tattoos—the kind that looked made with a ballpoint—sticking out of sleeveless tees. Their whole look was intimidating, which I guess was the point. My heart was racing. Adrenalin was moving, but I felt sorely inadequate to defend myself. This was their home turf; they were marching in the middle of the night as they approached this single old guy who looked like he might be easy pickin's.

They were almost on me. I had to do something. I stepped straight at them, causing them to stop, surprised, right in front of me. "Hey guys." I said. "I bet you're wondering what's going on down there with those boats." I pointed toward the three boats nearly invisible in the darkness and it was obvious that they didn't even know the boats existed until I pointed them out. They stared a moment with wide eyes and then the apparent leader turned back to me and said, "What are they doin' down there?"

I gave them a pretty good, but quick summary of WaterFire Sharon and put them in the middle of it. Sharon was their town, and it was going to make them proud. They listened and I could sense some of their energy and attention was diverted away from me. When I felt I could, I said "Well, I've got to hustle to get over there to time these guys . . . I'll see you later." I dashed quickly in the direction they came from, and toward a streetlight.

They spun on their heels, surprised at my abrupt movement and then hesitated. Their leader yelled sharply in a way that stopped me in my tracks . . .

"Hey **Mister.**

Thanks for talking to us!"

There Was No Art

7V. It was terrible. I've tried to forget as much of it as I can but that's where I was. In the seventh grade, in the Junior High School, in Cranston. 7V was a tracked group of somewhat matched-up students. Future gangsters, drug lords, prostitutes, car fatalities, etc., and it was where I would stay until I was 8V, and then 9V, unless something happened to me or I dropped out of school. High school felt a long way from 7V. I felt tracked for life.

The 7V Division was 20 students. We filled a classroom nicely and traveled together to all our basic studies. But teachers cringed when they saw us coming. We were the baddest kids in the school and everyone knew it. Now when I use the term "we", I mean to say I was in there, trapped in there somehow. I never did find out how I ended up there, but I must have had a bad testing day or something, and like most people claim in prison, "I am innocent!" But there I was. It was just the way things worked. Or didn't. Put all the troublemakers in one room together—good idea! Now, as I said, I was innocent, but in this group, I was painted with the same broad brush. The guys were trouble, and so were the girls . . . . maybe even worse, as instigators, the girls.

My memory of what we looked like was 'from another world'. The majority were 'Mondo'. Lots of black leather, with metal highlights, slicked back hair combed continually, leaving clear track marks from the ever-present pocket comb. The sides were combed back, the center was gently pulled forward, balanced and kept from falling all the way by a good dose of Brylcream that hardened up as it dried. Today it's "John, put your phone away." Back then is was "John, put your comb away." The shoes were black. Motorcycle boots were common, with the heels tacked to give a little click—like music when you walked down the hall. And the girls? Black fishnet stockings. Black, micro-miniskirts. Lots of make-up, dark around the eyes, crazy lips, and jewelry—often including some 'older guy's' class ring. It might be on a chain around her neck. Sometimes it was wrapped around the band with 20 feet of tape to keep it on a finger. I don't think I ever met one of those 'older' guys. Maybe they were out of school, working in a gas station. Or were doing time somewhere after killing some guy for talking to his girlfriend . . . hint, hint . . . but everyone knew who was spoken for. And like the comb for the guys, it was the teasing comb and brush for the girls. I suspect the parents of at least some of the girls would not have approved of the way their daughters coiffed and dressed, as the finishing touches came after they left the house. Hair was teased up into a huge nest, lightly smoothed on the outside and held in place by a cloud of hairspray that, on application, gagged everyone in the room. They all had a can in their big black leather handbags.

I recently watched the old film "Rebel Without a Cause" starring James Dean—they could have filled the cast with 'V' Division students. It was tough for me to watch because I saw the reality of the story, and even I was in there, playing a character I didn't want to be.

Junior High School certainly opened up a whole new world for me. School wasn't much about my classes. It was about a whole world order. I wasn't a 'Mondo', or a 'Colleege' or a 'Continental'. I stayed enough in between these types to just keep from getting roughed up or bullied. Invisibility was the key. The less I stood out, the more I was forgotten, the safer I was.

The 'V' Division worked every day to maintain its bad reputation. In all fairness, the whole school was trouble.

The administration was very creative in attempting to gain order with incredibly strict rules. We walked double file in the hall between classes with no talking. The lavatories were locked between classes so no groups could meet there. They made you beg a teacher to use the bathroom and sometimes the answer was no. To punish some bad behavior by some group, maybe even the 'V' Division, the whole school was punished. You ended up with enemies all over the place. All the teachers would be on guard, ready to cite violations. I hated that. The walk home, if I missed the bus because of detention, was over an hour, and in the winter, it would be dark before I got there. I know what a prison feels like. I was there, starting in the seventh grade, in 'V' Division.

I actually felt sort of sorry for our teachers, impossibly trying to do their job. That is until I became collateral damage when they lashed back at my class for bad behavior. I remember Geography. I liked Geography. One day I saw kids passing a note while the teacher, with his back turned, was writing on the board. It kind of went around without any particular destination until the teacher saw it. The passing note picked up speed from hand to hand as the teacher tried to grab it. The rows of desks and students became an obstacle course, and the teacher just chased the note, finally tipping the desks in the way—right over, on their sides to the floor, kids included. The whole class started screaming, especially the girls. The teacher finally caught up to the note, which was firmly held in the hand of Charlie, not a real bad kid. Charlie was on the floor, face down on his stomach, pinned by the teacher's foot square on his back as he twisted Charlie's arm behind him until Charlie screamed in pain and finally let the note go. When the teacher read the note, he went more berserk. A couple of kids ran for help while the rest of us were on our feet using the upturned furniture as a barricade and staying as far as possible away from the charging teacher. Finally help did arrive. The teacher was given a day off to cool down. We were all given detention. I later found out the note said, "Mr. So-and-So is a jerk." and it was intended to be lost to Mr. So-and-So. Just for 'V' Division fun.

Rarely did I personally represent trouble but there was a time in Science class that I dared to raise my hand, briefly coming out of invisibility. I said to the teacher that he was wrong about water conducting electricity. I had just read about the properties of 'pure' water in the textbook and I knew I was right. He must have already been on edge because he flipped. He lunged and chased me around the lab tables like he wanted to kill me, until I escaped out the back door and into the hall. Students and teachers stuck their heads in the hall yelling and cheering as we ran by. I arrived at the office just paces ahead of him. That was close, and of course I was suspended.

Another ugly memory I carry shows how really 'bad' "We" could be. For some reason, in the middle of the school year we got a brand new, young, very pretty, smiley, 'out to save the world', teacher. Just one day with our class made her quit and seek an alternative career. We never saw her again.

But by far, the strongest memory I have is of art class. I really couldn't believe my good fortune. I was so excited to be starting a class that would be so much fun—creativity and all that. We met once a week for the semester. The very first class the teacher was prepared for us—"We"—the baddest. She was tough. She read us our rights and responsibilities and assured us of swift, strong punishment if anyone gave her any kind of problem. I don't remember her even mentioning art in that first class, but I was excited and rarin' to go.

The very next class we filed in and took our seats. I was still excited, but the teacher didn't look happy. It seems someone had stolen a pair of scissors from her desk in our first class—or so she said—and she wanted them back. She said we would sit there for the entire period until someone confessed to the crime or told her who had stolen them. It was a long period. We were not allowed anything on our desktop. Our hands had to lie flat on its surface. No studying, no reading, no talking, no sleeping—for the entire period—and then this became every period for the entire semester. There was no art. We all flunked. She never got her scissors back. I never found out who stole them or even if they were ever really stolen.

So it went in 'V' Division. Even if you were innocent going in, just like prison you learned a lot while you were there, and it wasn't always good. Somehow, I survived. Barely. But life got better. And school got better too. Then one insightful high school teacher found me—

the real me—and became my champion. She guided me, convinced me first, and then other teachers, of my worth if given a chance. And maybe that is why I became a teacher. And maybe that is why I still today keep my eyes open to try to help that student who looks like a villain on the outside but . . . on the inside . . . looks . . . just like me.

Pulling a Maino

IT WAS AN UNUSUALLY COLD, DARK, MOONLESS, AUTUMN NIGHT. John Mongelli, Christine Maino, and I were putting WaterFire tender boats away after one of the last fires of the season. All the equipment had to be broken down and put away. The goal was to rid the site of all evidence of the many thousands of attendees from the night before. And it was always an impressive achievement. Or, was it a dream?

Except for the unusual low temps, it was a night like many others. At least that's what we expected. We stuck together with our boats and passed through the hurricane barrier. Except for our wake, the water was calm. We pushed the throttles forward like we never did when we were on the river. It was beautiful. Minutes later we slowed and aimed for the dock. It wasn't well-lit but we knew it well, having done the trip so many times. We made short work of the spring lines that we had to use to let the boats safely and securely rise and fall with the tides.

Christine finished tying up and stood back. She and I usually worked together, and we took turns as captain of our boat Prometheus. John was one of the first volunteer boat captains, if not the first, so between the three of us we had over sixty years experience behind the WaterFire wheel.

I finished next and stepped back, then glanced over at Christine. She was dressed in several layers for the cold. She took a step forward to the edge of the dock. And, then another step forward, out over the water—and—she went down. Feet first, without a sound, without a ripple. I couldn't believe what I saw. I kept looking but there was nothing to look at.

Christine was gone. Without a trace.

I jumped to the edge of the dock and yelled "John!"

I reached in the water and swirled as deep as I could but came up empty.

"John, Chris is gone. . . in the water." He looked at me like I was nuts, and looked around to see Christine, but she was really gone.

"Here, she went here." I yelled "Here!" John got the picture.

"Grab my feet" I yelled, and he did. I took a deep breath and lowered my head, arms and shoulders into the frigid dark water and swept my hands as far as I could reach in all directions.

Nothing! But I couldn't give up. If I came to the surface it was giving up on her. And there was no time to spare. I pulled against John to grab every inch of distance possible, and then something touched my hand. . . I grabbed at it, whatever it was. Was it hair? It could be hair, and I pulled as hard as I could, without pulling the hair right out of her head and losing her again. The layers of clothing were incredibly heavy under water, with Christine sandwiched in the middle. Then I found a piece of her coat. That was easier to manage, and I pulled her toward the surface as quick as I was able.

As soon as John saw her break the surface he jumped and grabbed her and pulled her tight against the dock. I joined him. It took both of us to pull her out of the water. We turned her onto her side, and then to her stomach and started to use long-ago-learned lifesaving techniques. Convulsions came suddenly, and the sea water gushed from her lungs and mouth and she came back to life—life that we were worried she had lost.

It was nothing short of a miracle. None of us, including Chris, knew why she walked off the dock. She didn't intend to. I was reminded of the Olympics diving competition, where you look for smooth entry in the water. She was perfect. She snapped out of her trance after she went under and struggled to get to the surface, but for all her effort, she just sank deeper in all her saturated layers of clothing. She gave up fighting the losing battle and was headed for the bottom. She told me later she just knew she was a goner, until she was pulled up on the dock.

Chris recovered quickly and refused a ride to the emergency room.

She even drove herself home that night, after changing into some dry clothes.

Everyone, of course, heard about it. John and I were considered lucky lifesavers of a sort. From that lesson, everyone out in the bay at night, had to actually "wear" a life vest. Chris became a household word, but by her last name. Anyone who fell in the water after that night was pulling a "Maino." A "Half-Maino" if you didn't go all the way under. The coined words even spread through our Kansas City and Sharon, Pennsylvania WaterFire volunteers. John and I were happy just to have been successful. As I said, it was a miracle.

Oh, and one last thing, Chris is famous for her chocolate chip cookies, and John and I have been getting a good share ever since.

Lessons from India

ONE DAY THIRTY PLUS YEARS AGO, I SAT ON A LONG WOODEN bench, worn smooth and slightly curved, subtly reflecting the different shapes of the many bodies, that through the decades, have waited there. The room was humid, warm and cavernous. What light there was, came from a few runs of stark fluorescent tubes attached to the high ceiling. Just below were several slow, soundless fans, slicing the thick air. The sounds I remember were voices foreign, and colorful, surrounding me in this old-world setting. The air there was filled with the scent of body oils, incense, and curry, as it is in all of India. Just outside the doors the sun shone strongly, but this was another world: an old world, of old British conquest, architecture, rules, and procedures.

I was trying to make an international phone call. These were the days before internet, cell phones, or even home phones in India. The central post office was the only place one could make an international call. It was a time consuming and complicated procedure you reserved only for special occasions, emergencies, or big business deals. I don't remember any more which it was for me. I only remember the sitting, and the passage of a great deal of time, with the company of so many people, waiting.

Among us were families, with babies and grandmothers in tow. There were girlfriends, young wives, and businessmen young and old. There were suits, and saris. Some displayed bindi, the painted forehead dots on women. Some had tiny bells sewn into light fabric that tinkled when they moved, and some wore heavy men's watches with loose oversized wrist bands that spoke of prosperity. And then, a few, like me, who wore a t-shirt, and well-traveled jeans.

The procedure was simple. You queued up at a window and

patiently gave all your call information and a deposit in rupees, to the telephone clerk. Then you took a seat and waited and waited for your name to be called. When it was, and if you recognized it as pronounced, you would spring up from the smooth bench and scurry into one of the wooden phone boxes fixed with a glass panel that allowed some light in and dampened some of the competing sounds of India around you.

I remember the setting. I remember the people. I especially remember one of the people already sitting there when I arrived. He was a young man, close to my age... slender, a bit scraggly, with longish hair, and thinly bearded. He could have been Indian. He may have been a Sikh without his turban. He could well have been a Middle Eastern traveler. He could have been anybody. I'm sorry I didn't get his name. But whoever he was, he sat next to the last free seat in the waiting area. And whatever he was, it was not just his attire that spoke for him. It was also his demeanor. He quietly projected a cool, inner strength. Everyone seemed to sense his seriousness and kept a certain distance. Perhaps that was why the space next to him was still up for grabs. He hardly acknowledged the existence of others in the waiting area, including me, though we sat close but not touching each other on the long wooden bench. Eventually I tried to be friendly, saying something small to him like "This takes forever. Eh?" Except for a side glance, in my general direction, he didn't respond. I didn't even know if he spoke English, but I had found that most people did to some degree, especially in India. He just wasn't sociable. More time passed and I tried again with another simple question like "Are you Indian"? He actually turned to me this time and said "No." and turned back. Determined to break the ice I asked, "Where then, do you come from?" He mumbled something I couldn't understand, and I think that was his intention.

Being a bit of a young and brassy and maybe repulsive American, I was determined to engage in a simple conversation so I switched to what I thought might be a safer topic. I asked him about the T-shirt he wore. I had been trying to make out something in black letters on his shirt front, but I couldn't quite read it. The shirt wasn't new. It was white, clean, worn thin with tiny holes starting to appear, probably from rough laundering on rocks at the side of a river, as was the practice there. It was the message it carried that gave it value, and probably made a statement for him. In effect, his attire was speaking for him. In answer he simply turned frontwards so I could read it for myself.

"How do we get the Russians out?" Just a question. . . in English. "How do we get the Russians out?"

Then he turned and showed me the back. It had an upper body print of a uniformed Russian soldier with a rifle strapped on his back, holding a chium to his mouth. The chium was the pipe they used over there to smoke hashish and opium. The caption below the soldier, and the answer to the question on the shirt's front panel said, "We smoke them out."

"How do we get the Russians out? We smoke 'em out."

I thought it was interesting, but I didn't understand the meaning. It was then, for some reason, he decided I was harmless, and he opened up to me. He patiently, carefully, and quietly explained the meaning to this young dumb American that there was a war going on, and not that far away.

He'd come overland from Afghanistan, across Pakistan, to India to help in the war against Russia. The Russians held Afghanistan hostage. (His English was really, quite good and getting better as he relaxed.) So he was not really a soldier, but he had been doing his part to help liberate Afghanistan. He explained that it was a tough country in many ways but had suffered through the ages at the hands of greater military powers seizing control of the mountains, plains, and plateaus that were the rugged nation of Afghanistan. A nation of strong tribal tradition but weak central control. A nation that could be taken but not held. His part was not that of a foot soldier, although I could see him as one. He was a sort of courier. A rebel in another way. He had traveled to India, carrying semi-precious gems, like lapis lazuli. He then had me peek into his bag, as he held it so no one else could see. I saw a sandwich-size chunk of blue stone, resting atop others, a bit rough, but probably valuable. India was a wide-open market. He traded these gems commonly mined in Afghanistan for good American dollars, the international currency. The dollars traveled back to Afghanistan with him and eventually supported the farmers, growers of hashish and most important, the poppy. Russian soldiers, deprived of their vodka from home, easily fell victim to other diversions, and the growers of hashish and opium were more than happy to fill the bill, at very low prices; sometimes even trading opium for valuable "misplaced" Russian weapons. The Afghan residents may have been no match in military power, but the longer the resistance kept up, the more demoralized the Russian soldiers became. He said the Russian Army was losing its 'will to fight' and Russia was going broke in the process.

My well-spoken, now apparently well-educated, friend had given me a picture of a world not far away but one that I hardly knew existed. My name was finally called by the telephone clerk and I was reminded of the reason I was there. I sprinted into the ancient phone booth and talked to somebody back in the U.S. about something. I no longer remember with whom, or about what. It wasn't the phone call I remember at all. It was meeting the young man whose mission was to change the world. I just wanted to see it. When I came out of the telephone booth, I discovered my 'freedom fighter' was gone. He might have made his call from another booth and left quickly, or maybe he felt like he had drawn too much attention to himself to be safe and had to leave. I don't know. He was just gone. It was like a dream you wake up from and wonder if it really happened. He, and his interesting 'Smoke 'em out' t-shirt, his bag full of semi-precious gems, and most of all, the Russian story he told me, delivered in a very serious, careful manner. From that day forward, whenever I heard mention of news from Afghanistan, I paid attention. I had learned something new and important to the world we lived in.

But, little by little I forgot about my Indian post office encounter. It wasn't until 9/11 when the entire world watched buildings collapse, and many thousands of Americans murdered that certain old memories came to the surface. Things I hadn't thought about for a long time. And there was one magazine cover that just did me in. I stared at it for the longest time—until it finally stared back at me. As if to say, "What did you expect?" It gave me a chill.

Although time does have a way of twisting things, my memory brought me clearly back to the post office that day. The bench worn smooth. The fragrances and families. The overhead fan that sliced the hot and humid air. The gems, and a t-shirt that said it all, and most notably, the lesson about Afghanistan by a teacher without a name.

The world has indeed changed, but little is new. The Russians were driven out of Afghanistan. The Americans moved in, and the conflict continues. And I have to wonder, who was the young intelligent, well-educated, English-speaking individual who gave me a lesson about the turmoil there.

Sometimes the mind plays tricks on us, but sometimes it just tells us the truth. A truth however difficult to fully accept, may still be the truth. In this case, I'm just left to wonder.

Come Fly with Me

HAVE YOU EVER TRIED TALKING TO SOMEONE ONLY TO DISCOVER they're wearing earphones, connected to a cell phone, and have no clue of your existence, never mind hear what you said to them? I even apologize for the possible invasion. I'm trying to break that habit. . . the apology. I actually feel a little sorry for them. Even in the plane literally rubbing up against them, as you do in the cheap seats, you still find those who have built a wall, to keep themselves in, and keep others out. *So sorry.*

I love to travel. Just being in an airport is exciting. I spend my time observing all the different kinds of people you find there—those meeting a flight, or those just seeing someone off. I used to play a little game of "made it, married it, or inherited it." I would size up the passengers, who were always well dressed back in the day. I tried to determine which category they fell into by how they looked, and the kind of contact they seemed to have with fellow passengers and family. My favorites where the ones I put in the "made it" category. Appeared confident, but not haughty, and gave the impression if they lost everything, they could just do it again. It's a little tougher to play this game today. It is not just the rich that fly. Everyone dresses down, not up. And then there's that group behind the wall, a wall of their own choice, to keep others, others like me, out.

But I still try. My last trip went like this . . . Providence to Newark, Newark to Pittsburgh, Pittsburgh to Washington, Washington to Providence. In Newark, waiting for my connecting flight, I was very early, so I sat observing people while alternately thumbing through a flight magazine I had picked up earlier. I was looking for a diversion, when I saw a young woman, maybe early 20's, with a couple small carry-ons. She scanned around a bit, seeming a little unsure of herself. There were plenty of places to sit but she picked a seat just two away from me. Her casual style of dress, sandals, and skin color told me she was not from 'round these parts.' Oh yeah, I also love to guess people's nationalities and have gotten pretty good at it. I didn't want to scare her away, but I hoped she might say something to me, and start some friendly chat.

She looked my way. I caught her eye, and just said "Hi". That's how it started. It's just an invitation, if you need one. And she did. She was puzzled. "Why are there not more passengers waiting for the Pittsburgh flight?" I answered "it was too early but surely many more would be there soon." Her accent. . . I'm guessing India, or. . . maybe Pakistan but not as likely. So I asked. I always do it the same way. I say "I hear just a little bit of an accent in your voice." I say this no matter how bad their English, or how strong their accent. Very, very few have any reservation in telling me where they are from and "Bingo" she was from India. I spent a month there once. We were deep in conversation when an airline rep came up to us to say they have changed gates for Pittsburgh, and we had to move. We walked together and talked. At the new gate, we met up with all the missing passengers but still had time to waste. She then asked me if my love for India extended to Indian food. It seemed when I met her, she was fresh off her Air India flight, from Mumbai. She opened one of the two bags her mother had given her before she boarded. She withdrew container after container of her mother's specialties, and we tasted them all. Long distance take-out from India. It was delicious and by then we were pretty good friends.

This was her first trip to the USA. She was a little nervous, but excited, and she said she enjoyed talking to me. I felt the same. In a few days she was starting school at Carnegie Mellon in Pittsburgh. A very bright young woman. We exchanged contact info and promised to stay in touch from time to time. When we finally boarded, and found our separate seats, we both knew. We were like the "two ships passing in the night"—separated by many miles, and many years.

On the next leg I sat next to a middle-aged man, well-groomed, dressed very well, all in black. He was silent. He didn't make an attempt to speak with me for a couple minutes but, after checking his ears for ear buds, I asked him if he minded the open window shade. It was very bright, but I like to see where we're going. He was fine, and we each threw in a little small talk. His accent . . . slight, but I could hear a bit of British in there somewhere. That's always tough because the Brits were masters of introducing beer, and the English language, around the world. I asked him my standard question of accents and nationality. He looked at me and said with pride, "born and raised in Pittsburgh. . . and that's where I'm going right now to visit my family." Wow, I was way off on that one! Or I thought so, until we chatted about careers. It seems he is, and has been for the last 15 years, professor of economics, at university, in Glasgow, Scotland. He couldn't help but pick up a little accent. He doesn't like scotch.

Will and I discussed the probable economic future of England due to British withdrawal from the EEC, and the recent attempted but unsuccessful withdrawal and independence for Scotland from England. He also drew parallels to the American presidential elections coming up soon. As he said, "Sometimes unexpected things do happen, and people wake up. . . but too late." We got into favorite books, and films, and hardly noticed the time when we hit the tarmac in Pittsburgh. We've since swapped a couple emails of "things I forgot to tell you." And "don't forget, when you come to Scotland, my castle is your castle", etc.

A chance acquaintance I made while filing down the chute to the airplane in Newark was with Jeff. All I did was turn around to see who was complaining about something. This rather small man with long hair and a vertical striped, multicolored shirt looked at me, because I was the only one listening, and told me his tale of woe. It seems he had been trying to get home for two days and he was paying someone to take his place at work. A mechanical problem was the reason why his first flight was grounded. He said they put him up in a very nice room in a very nice hotel, but he had to get home. The second day's flight was canceled due to weather, and they didn't pay this one because it was weather related. . . lots of storms around. We were right then boarding his home leg flight, but he said, "I'll believe it when I see it." He was so worked up he finally apologized to the passengers close to him. He said "I'm really not usually like this. I get along with everyone. I'm a people person." I asked him what kind of work he was in. . . and he stepped back and stared at me. Then he stepped forward. He spoke softly. "I'm an embalmer. I've been embalming people for 35 years." Ah ha—no customer complaints

I appreciate a good-looking person. There are lots of factors here that make it so. And certainly plenty of room for how we might define good looking. When I was doing a little people watching before my flight from Pittsburg to Washington, my long-distance vision caught sight of an extraordinary beautiful woman. Maybe 5'6". Dark but healthy-complexioned from time spent outside. Dark chestnut hair. Gorgeous legs and arms surrounded by a blouse and shorts that did nothing but compliment her. She didn't have too much of anything, but she certainly didn't lack anything either.

I actually first spotted her up just ahead of me as I was entering the terminal. She was a pleasure to watch. Even the way she walked was beautiful. I could see as I followed that other people noticed her too. How could they not? I adjusted my pace to follow her at a reasonable distance. At least for the moment we were heading in the same direction.

And then, she entered a rest room. Shoot! I actually considered hanging around and picking up her trail again later. I had time but it felt like stalking and I just kept going. I had my treat. But I would not soon forget such a remarkable beauty!

In Washington I had another wait for the Providence flight. I sat patiently at the last seat to the corridor at the gate. . . more people watching. Way, way down the terminal walkway, maybe 30 gates away, I spotted a splash of color. It was the same color I had seen earlier on the incredibly beautiful woman in Pittsburgh. It came in and out of sight as the many people between walked and ran and stood around looking at departure screens. But as the color came closer, I knew it was the same. The same colors, the same beauty, the same graceful movement, getting closer and closer, and finally to the point where I could no longer look, because she would see me staring at her as she approached. I looked down at the boarding pass in my hand, and from my peripheral vision saw that she had just seated herself, right next to me. Whew!

It took a moment to gain the courage and just look up, and to the side. Gorgeous! And she turned to me and smiled. It was time to say something. My mouth opened but my brain hadn't put anything there to let out. I was immediately destroyed when I heard myself say, "Nice tan!" But instead of turning away or changing her seat, she said "Oh, that's from watching lots of little league games that my 3 sons play in." I thought well, that's nice, and she's giving me the "Don't even try, I'm married" line, without actually having to say it. But then she said, "I've done a lot of that since my divorce."

Kathy and I talked and talked. Her heritage is Scottish and English, but I couldn't believe it. She said "Yeah, nobody does." She was on her way to Providence and was on the Pittsburgh flight, but I hadn't seen her. She worked for State Farm Insurance in Pittsburgh but they were closing her office and shuffling staff to other sites around the country. They would move her but with three kids in school she didn't want to go anywhere at least until her youngest, the 13-year-old, graduated from high school. She was on her way for a job interview at the head office of Amica Insurance, which was opening a new branch in Pittsburgh. It was her first job interview in many years, and she was very nervous. I have Amica insurance. I used to teach job interview skills to high school students. I have studied Amica customer service policies and used them in case studies. I had lots of information for her to use in her interview. She took out her iPad and got it all down. Even recognizing the little bit of psychology about their annual Thanksgiving cards, instead of Christmas cards. She loved that!

Well, that was quite an encounter. We boarded and found our separate seats. I hope she did well in her interview. Just another two ships passing in the night thing. . . .

That experience would have been hard to beat on my last leg home. And when I sat down in my seat, my seat companion did not look up. I was about to say something to him, a young guy, when I noticed the ear buds, connected to his cell phone, that made a wall, that he built for himself, that I would leave intact for him. So sorry!

"Follow the Yellow Brick Road"

PART 1

WE LEARNED A LOT BY MEETING AND TALKING WITH FELLOW travelers. It's surprising how many there are. Our guidebook was *Southeast Asia on a Shoestring* and everyone used it. We even met some of the same people again and again in different countries because we used the same guidebook. Our common route was known by all as "The Yellow Brick Road." Partly for the quest we shared, but mostly because the guidebook was yellow. We did some research and found that the cheapest way to get to Bali, Indonesia from Singapore, was with two boats. The first leg was a privately-owned fishing boat. It would take us to an island named Tanjun Pinang, about a third of the way to Jakarta. There we would board the *Batu Hari ll*, the brand-new ferry that replaced the *Batu Hari* which had been taken out of service and sent off for scrap. That one was reputedly a dirty, stinking, uncomfortable, unsafe, rust bucket that, with only a 'wing and a prayer', completed its weekly trip back and forth between the two major ports. But it was no longer in service. We could relax.

We teamed up with a few other "round the world" backpackers to make a full boat and got an early start the next day—and it was beautiful. But, after about four hours, we ran into a problem. The problem was the Indonesian Coast Guard. They pulled us over and lashed our two boats together. We were many miles from anywhere. We tried to talk but were not allowed to even ask a question. Instead we sat together on the hot steel deck and stared at them—actually, two of them—the ones with automatic weapons and jumpy hands pointed in our direction. We were their prisoners, and just sat there, maybe a few miles north of the equator, quietly rolling from side to side in the swell of the Java Sea. Our passports were taken and disappeared with the two captains who had walked around back of the wheelhouse for a little privacy. Were we scared? You bet! Our captain, bargaining on our behalf, explained we had to pay a small fine, for something or other that was illegal. It came to about 12 dollars, per person. Cash. We were sure it was a scam, worked regularly, to earn a few extra dollars. Our captain was probably right in on it. I tried to snap a picture of the bunch of us being held at gunpoint—and nearly lost my camera. I did lose my film, but better than losing my life. It got heated for a moment. We were quite relieved and happy when they finally let us go. We realized several times on our world trip, if something happened to us, our friends and relatives would not even have known where to start looking for us. We could have just disappeared without a clue. When we were underway again, we felt lucky to just be alive.

We arrived at our island destination Tanjun Penang and learned we had another problem. The boat we intended to take to Jakarta, the only boat to Jakarta from there, was reported to have sunk. The *Batu Hari ll* was new and put in service recently to replace the ancient rust bucket, *Batu Hari*. Over 100 passengers and crew on the new boat had perished, along with our only transportation to Jakarta. We most fortunately had missed the enormous tragedy. But our brief stop was replaced by an indefinite stay on Tanjun Penang. We scrambled looking for any kind of place to stay, but Tanjun Penang was anything but a tourist destination. We were lucky to find a shack with a thatched roof poised on a pier in the bay, a few feet over the water.

It was water at high tide, and mud flats at low tide. Lots of families lived like this. Our neighbors were not especially friendly and spoke no English; therefore, we had to learn how to do things on our own. Simple things like the toilet. We didn't actually have a toilet. What we did have was a piece of plywood that covered a hole sawn in the floor in our hut. It was flushed automatically at high tide. At low tide it was the realm of big rats that sloshed noisily through the muck looking for treats. The mosquitoes were a bigger problem and it was times like those I'm sure we got our money's worth from the typhoid shots and malaria pills we got in San Francisco. Babies cried, rats sloshed, insects hummed. We read and swatted by candlelight, deep into the hot night, not willing to give in to the relentless mosquitos, and we wondered how, and when, we were ever going to get out of there. We kept asking island officials when we might see a boat. And, because they had to tell us something, they kept answering "tomorrow." This they told us, with some degree of certainty, day after day.

But our stay wasn't bad. We met a few interesting natives and 'yellow brick road' travelers, all waiting 'for the same boat' (the only boat), that we were. The food was good, and cheap. Being right on the equator, and at sea level, the weather was sunny, hot and humid, interrupted by an occasional downpour. In the evenings, most of the island's life became apparent—when it cooled off a bit. The natives energized and I distinctly remember the land crabs caught running around on the beach and later cooked and sold from vendors' baskets. (I would highly recommend the crabs caught on the high tide.) Lanterns hung from posts on their carts and gave everything a magical glow. We were settled as best we could. We had no choice. We spent our time walking, reading, sleeping, eating and practicing Indonesian phrases from our guidebook *Southeast Asia on a Shoestring*. We often heard phrases like "Tidak apa apa", meaning "no problems."

A few days later, people began yelling to each other there was a boat coming. It was a boat bound for Jakarta, and it was big enough to take everyone—maybe. We grabbed our stuff and hurried to a big boat pier along with what looked like hundreds of others with the same thing in mind. It was going to be a battle, and we would have to compete by pushing and shoving to make sure we four were among those to make it on the ship. The ship by the way was the *Batu Hari*— the first one—the one they had condemned and put in mothballs, only to be freed again. But there it sat in the rolling sea, far enough out to float freely above the bottom, just waiting to take us on the next leg of our journey, the next leg of our adventure.

The boat was huge, but nowhere near shore where we all stood waiting in the hot sun for the it to come in. It was at least a mile out to sea and rumor quickly spread it might not come in at all. We waited, and watched, and watched each other. More than once we found hands in our pockets that were not our own, and spotted razor blades hidden in native hands, waiting for an opportunity to slit a pack or money belt. Slit, grab, run! Our guidebook had warned us. Jimi and I fortunately had learned to be tough and acted much tougher than we actually were. We managed to keep the problem in check, mainly by watching for potential problems, before they were attempted. Our eyes, and cold stares were warning— "Don't even think about it."

When we no longer believed we were going anywhere on that *Batu Hari,* an unbelievable craft appeared out of nowhere. It was a barge lashed to what looked to be a fishing boat and it was almost big enough to hold all the would-be passengers. It was lower than the pier and as soon as it was jockeyed alongside, the passengers started throwing their bags, and boxes, and finally themselves down to the mangled deck of the barge, like it was the last helicopter out of Vietnam. There were a few small injuries—cuts and bruises from being walked over, or knocked over, or landing wrong when jumping down, or children slipping from adult grips down to the deck of the barge. But we four were good. We were on the barge, and though a little roughed up by the experience, we were finally getting somewhere.

It was a slow passage out to the *Batu Hari.* The barge was just a barge after all. To power us out all we had was the engine in the fishing boat. And the Java Sea was rougher than it looked from shore. Already, people not used to the sea were starting to get sick. In such close quarters, throwing-up was contagious, and squeezing to the rail to get sick over the side? There was no rail. It was not even an option. If you didn't fall overboard, you would lose your possessions to thieves as soon as you left them unattended. Those who needed to, just threw up in place, starting a chain reaction.

The *Batu Hari* got closer as we slowly plowed out until we finally just crashed into it, side to side in the huge swells. An enormous net, like a 20- or 30-foot rope ladder, had been hung over the side of it. Up and down we went, crashing. It was like a pirate movie. The younger, more agile of the men started leaping the gap, grasping the net, quickly climbing up to the deck and disappearing from our sight. I watched as our two craft rose and fell and banged horribly together with each swell. I expected to see bodies falling from the net, crushed with the impact, finally vanishing forever under the white water between us. We watched, we studied, we planned how to do it—like our lives depended on it—which they did.

Fran and Jimi, Sue and I, waited for a milder moment in the sea. As quickly as possible with our packs on our backs, we leaped, caught the net and climbed up the rope netting like monkeys, watching out for each other.

When we came to the rail, we saw that every inch of the boat was covered by humanity. The boat was apparently full before it had even arrived. We looked everywhere for a place to sit, or lay, if we were lucky, on the deck. We stepped on people as we searched for a spot, and finally found a little space that others had rejected for some reason.

When the anchor was raised and we got underway, we realized why. The ancient boat that was to be our home for the next couple of days, started to roll differently once it moved further from shore into the deeper sea. And with every roll, a generous stream—a small wave actually—of urine and feces and cheap toilet paper ankle deep, swirled over the threshold of the restroom, a few feet away. And with each heave, the heavy rusty, steel restroom door swung open, and then closed with a big crash. Our lucky little space turned out to be too good to be true. A ship has to be pretty bad to go to mothballs, and maintenance of the little things would not have been a priority. "Tidak apa apa." We found a drier spot and we took turns guarding it or walking around to see what the ship provided for amenities. Below decks, the entire massive hold was filled with human beings. The only light came from the same gas lanterns we saw everywhere, that cast that warm glow over the multitude of faces—which all stared at us. There was some food being offered for sale, but in the dank hold, everything smelled like bilge water. We were pleasantly surprised to learn that a meal of sorts was being served on deck at the bow of the ship. They had cleared a few square feet of the steel deck and started a fire under a propped-up 50-gallon steel drum. We got there just in time to see the first tastes by patrons, holding flimsy plastic bowls, of freshly-prepared fish head soup.

But the soup apparently did not meet expectations and with just one taste, these patrons, all of them, worked their way to the rail, and just hummed the whole thing overboard, flimsy plastic bowl and all. Their faces told us all we needed to know—sick, disappointed faces. We decided to pass and walked back to the hold where we bought a big bunch of bananas—enough we figured, to last us the entire passage to Jakarta.

This was proving to be an interesting leg of our world journey. When we arrived at port, we stood at the rail and watched the whole mooring process, and even gave a little wave of congratulations to the wheelhouse, where there was undoubtedly a captain of great skill, and even greater courage. It had been so difficult to get on that ship, yet we found ourselves hesitating to get off, and step into the unknown of Jakarta. Thankfully, we had our yellow guidebook—on our way again, down the Yellow Brick Road.

It was then and there at the rail that we met a young man. A native who spoke English very well. He was happy to practice on us, and he gave us some tips on how to handle Jakarta, and Indonesia as a whole. He said, sternly, we could not be too careful! Especially in Jakarta. He was fascinated by us and asked lots of questions about the details of our trip and especially what lay ahead. Maybe someday we'd meet again. And with that, our new friend Bebang Sopany walked away, down the gangway, out of sight, and out of mind.

PART 2

WE CLEARED IMMIGRATION IN JAKARTA WHICH ACTIVATED OUR 30-DAY visas. Thirty days can go slow, or fast, depending on circumstances. We couldn't predict the future, but we were off and running. Running off to Bali, with stops en route for which we had contacts. The main one was with distant relatives by marriage with Fran's brother-in-law,

Albert. He had relatives in Bandung. Bandung is the intellectual capital of Java, maybe of the entire country of Indonesia. All the best schools are there. We were lucky for the contact. We needed a place to rest for a few days after our grueling cruise from Singapore. We called and as hoped, were given an invitation to visit the G*** family. The easiest, and cheapest form of transport was by bus. We started immediately and arrived in Bandung the next day, collapsing into the welcoming arms of Mr. and Mrs. G***, or just Mr. and Mrs. "Go", as they liked to be called. The house was a busy place with two teenage kids and a workforce of six or seven Javanese women, busy making and screening T shirts. The Go family lived and worked under the same roof, and they seemed to be living pretty well. We were treated like royalty. They cleaned us up (we needed it). They fed us heartily. They entertained us and told wonderful stories of the life they lived through their years in Indonesia. Our first night we politely listened to one of Mr. Go's stories of how his family, of Chinese descent, survived and prospered under difficult circumstances.

The previous president of Indonesia, Sukarno, held his power forcefully, and although a democracy, he systematically eliminated opponents by deadly means. Suharto was a popular opponent that Sukarno had to worry about. During the leadup to the election, the G*** family, at great risk, hid the future president of Indonesia, a young man at that time, in their home, and surely saved his life. One member of the family was given a high position in the Suharto cabinet, as Minister of Finance. This was unusual for someone of Chinese descent as they suffered systemic discrimination like minorities everywhere. This position in the government put him in charge of the purse strings, and he was said to be the second most powerful man in the country, second only to the President himself.

We sat on a soft overstuffed couch as he told the story that first evening. We could imagine the risks they took, the fear they experienced. We were given the image of them being discovered, and Sukarno's police scaling the high protective cement walls, topped with broken glass, that surrounded their house, and just killing everyone inside. As Mr. and Mrs. Go wound up the story, they realized we were falling asleep out of sheer exhaustion. We were led to our beds in various places. I was given a small room of my own that opened to a central hallway and within minutes I was out cold.

The next thing I knew, Sukarno's secret police smashed through the walls, shouting, glass flying everywhere with ear-shattering effects. I leaped up, and out of the bed, and tumbled onto the tile floor, cutting my knees and hands with the glass shards. A sudden light blinded me, causing me to face what I thought was certain death.

And there was Mr. Go grabbing me, trying to hold me and bring me back to consciousness, back to life—back to reality. Half asleep while earlier listening to the story, it seems I had carried it to my dreams. And Mr. Go, thinking he was doing me a favor as I slept, tried to close a glass louvered window that was just inches from my head. One of the glass panes slipped its frame and exploded on the tile floor. It took some moments to realize it was only a dream, and Mr. Go wasn't a storm trooper.

This was very embarrassing for all of us...but especially me. The whole house was up. But the cuts were minor, and I was soon back in bed and once again, out like a light.

Our timing, although accidental, was excellent. We had arrived just before Christmas. The majority of Indonesians are Muslims, a significant number are Hindu, and a small but tight group are Christian. As part of the Go family, we were invited to a midnight mass at the Catholic church. It was filled to the brim with a congregation dressed in its finest. It was unlike any other Catholic service I had been to, but most of my previous exposure was limited to weddings and funerals. This was truly a happy event and so strange to find while visiting Bandung.

After the service, Mr. Go treated us to a fine meal in a Chinese restaurant. I later learned that Chinese restaurants are famous for being open on other people's holidays. Mr. Go did the ordering, and it was an experience. I especially remember the tiny sparrow-sized birds, cooked whole and swimming in a delicious sauce. We were shown how to eat every last morsel, even crunching through the skull and chewing all the tiny bones.

On the ride home, in the middle of the night by this time, we passed a food vendor on the side of the road. Mr. Go abruptly turned around and bought several large pieces of fruit he called durian. When we arrived home, we still did not go to bed but went to the kitchen and were given a lesson on what to do with durian. We all sat on the floor in a circle looking at each other. Each of us was given one of these strange fruits. We took off our shoes and socks and used our feet to hold the fruits securely as we pulled them apart with our fingers. Durian have many cells about the size of medium eggs. Each cell has a consistency of soft cheese encircling a big seed. The flavor is unique. It might be described as an acquired taste. It is not the flavor or odor of dirty feet, but it's close, and some people complain. Later I started to notice in hotels, buses, and other public places, "No Durian Allowed" signs with pictures of durian with a big X over them. It is not a fruit for public consumption.

We learned a lot about Indonesia. We went with the Gos to visit the relative, who helped Suharto, who became the Finance Minister, who became incredibly wealthy. We met him at his weekend country estate which was huge. The entire estate was enclosed by tall walls with walk-ways and watch towers manned with guards and lots of machine guns. It was very much like a prison, but in this case kept people out, not in. The gates opened for us and we were met at the main doorway of the palace sandwiched between rice paddies and badminton courts. There was a helicopter sitting idle near the front door. The Minister came out to greet us and welcome us to his weekend home. He gave us a tour of the incredible property and were soon directed inside where he offered us conversation and cocktails. The room was cavernous, and cool. We sat on marble steps that lead directly to a small river diverted to run right through his house. A servant soon came pushing a portable bar with everything you could imagine and many things I'd never heard of. I remember trying the 50-year-old Chivas Regal, just for the fun of it. After several hours of chit-chatting, the Minister quietly took me aside to ask me a question. He wanted to know what I thought about how much money he needed to maintain his lifestyle, outside the country of Indonesia. There was no way I could answer that and told him so. He then asked, more specifically how far I thought he could get on 53 million dollars, which was the total of all he had, outside Indonesia. I took a wild guess and told him "probably pretty far." He told me he owned small pieces of over 150 companies licensed in Indonesia which would become worthless if he lost his position. But he also held lots of real estate in Europe and the U.S that he didn't even count. He knew his days were numbered. And so were Suharto's. They would probably go together, and not by choice. Hence the helicopter parked out front. It followed he and his family everywhere, ready to safely whisk them away to a new life when the time came.

During our visit, we got to know the Go kids better and did some stuff just for fun. The son took me out one day on his motor bike to the Japanese caves built during WWII, and then scorpion hunting. Both were new to me and both interesting.

Another first were massages. An experienced Javanese woman gave us each as much punishment as we could stand. Mrs. Go gave up her regular appointment so we could experience the "coin massage." The masseuse scraped each of us with a large old coin until we were sore and each of our ribs was visible and red—perhaps from bursting blood vessels.

It soon came time to leave our hosts and Bandung. We boarded a long-distance bus which stopped in Jogjakarta, famous for its batiks. While there, we each took a lesson from one of the better artists and learned the basics. We drew and painted and waxed and learned to create while sitting near a giant pot of boiling water over a wood fire in the jungle.

The next bus took us to the eastern shore of Java where we switched transportation to the ferry for the short ride across a strait. There we were met by some 15 or 20 kids swimming and diving in the clear aquamarine water for the coins that were flung out to them by passengers. We took one more bus to the famous Kuta Beach and made ourselves at home on the beautiful island of Bali.

Bali is geared toward tourism, especially the Australian market, being so close, inexpensive and safe. It's an easy place to be. We spent most of our days stretched out on the beautiful beach. The beach was the center of it all, and lovely Balinese girls, dressed of course in batik sarongs with big baskets balanced on their heads, brought us everything we needed, like fresh sliced fruits and fruit juices. My favorite vendor was Putu. She had the best offerings, including full body massage with exotic oils. Sometimes other girls would stop and offer massage, but I always told them "No thank you, Putu is our girl." Once, this simple statement brought a somewhat violent reaction, and caused the other woman to yell "Putu, Putu...that all I hear!" Putu was wonderful, and worth every cent of the dollar she charged.

But my favorite time on the beach was sunrise. It was beautiful and quiet except for the rolling surf that met the beach and seemed more like music as the sun rose up over the land behind me. And of course, there were the dancers. Fishermen actually, reminiscent of dancers, wading hip deep in the water, gracefully, expectantly, casting their throw nets into the surf.

Being first on the beach in early morning had other rewards as well. The best shells brought up in the night by the tides lay waiting to be discovered, and sometimes other things. My favorite find, which I have to this day, is a small, simple clay pot, the type often seen used as a teacup. Made by hand, fired without glazing—just a simple red clay cup. It was probably used once, and tossed away having fulfilled its purpose somewhere, to finally end up lying there in the wash of sand before my bare feet.

Bali was a paradise for us, but time was growing short. Our 30-day visas were closing in on us and we had to go back to Jakarta once again to board a boat and return to Singapore. On our last day, stretched out on the beach, we were brought to attention by the presence of a young man who approached us with familiarity. He was all smiles and we quickly realized we had met before. We had met on the *Batu Hari* standing at the rail just before disembarking. It was almost too strange to believe but fun at the same time. What a coincidence! He had some important reason to go to Bali, and everyone goes to Kuta Beach, and there we were, like old friends. We had forgotten about him, but we still had his Jakarta phone number and address, and we promised to call as soon as we arrived. He offered help to arrange cheap passage to Singapore and maybe housing until our departure. This was almost too good to be true.

Meeting Bebang Sopany was a stroke of luck, if there ever was one.

We left the next day, on the first long-distance bus out. We had two bus drivers and tickets all the way across Java to Jakarta. We slept in our seats, eating whenever we had the chance at rest stops and stared out, day and night, at an endless jungle, as the world passed us by.

PART 3

WE ARRIVED IN JAKARTA IN THE EARLY MORNING, WHICH IS A GOOD thing because it gives you all day to figure out what you are doing. We were not sure if our new friend Bebang was back yet from Bali, but we gave him a call and to our surprise he picked up. We told him we had just arrived and were near the bus station, which is a *really sleazy* area. He told us to stay put and he would come and meet us. We waited for what seemed like quite a while, but we didn't know how far away he lived. We certainly weren't going to complain about someone doing us a big favor. So we waited and were happy to see his face, although he looked a little haggard for some reason. He then explained that his mother had done something or other with somebody, and his house was unfortunately not available for us to use. But he would find us a cheap place to stay, and it would only be for one night because the *Batu Hari*, still floating, was leaving the next day at 5 p.m. He would help get us cheap tickets today and tomorrow we would sail. Things were getting a little complicated but, once again, we couldn't look a gift horse in the mouth. He led us down the street, and even helped carry our packs.

We stopped in front of a particularly unsavory looking storefront that had a hand made sign that said hotel. Bebang said this was a good friend of his and would give us a really good price. "Wait here." We waited and waited and when we looked in to see what was happening, he appeared to be in some kind of argument with another young guy behind the counter. It looked like their friendship was under stress to say the least. But he came out and said we had a room, he was sorry about the mess, and he was paying for it. "Don't worry. Standing by 100%" was what he said, and it wasn't the last time we heard it.

We entered the hotel, climbed a few flights of stairs and were dumbstruck by what we saw. Each floor was open, almost like a factory or a warehouse. There were no rooms as such. There were spaces cordoned off by chain link fencing. Some of the spaces had curtains or sheets tied up to block the view inside. There were cots, not beds, with no sheets or blankets. We were given a padlock to lock the door. We didn't know what to do. Fran and Sue were especially concerned. Bebang said, "Don't worry." It was only one night, and tomorrow we'd be gone. He calmed us down and we sat on the badly stained mattresses. We unpacked a little—as little as possible—including leaving Fran's diary on the bed. We all kept diaries of the trip, and notes of the people we met. Bebang had written his name, address, and telephone number in Fran's the very first time we met him, standing by the rail of the *Batu Hari*. But we were not comfortable.

Bebang then walked us around the neighborhood and explained that his uncle lived nearby, and he wanted to visit him so he could meet us. We did just that, through the maze of Jakarta; its alleys, shops, food carts, and sewers. We had no clue where we were, but we entered a little home and were instantly welcomed. We sat at a large table with the large family and just listened to the Indonesian, the only language we heard. Occasionally, Bebang would translate a sentence for our benefit and the whole family was impressed with his ability. We left shortly afterwards and walked back in the same kind a twisted journey that had brought us to his uncle's.

Bebang had a vehicle. It was a motor scooter and his plan was to leave Sue and Fran in the "hotel" to wait for us, while Jimi and I hung tight to Bebang as he drove us to meet his friend at the port shipping offices. The friend who could definitely get us tickets, even if there were no more tickets available, and at a very good price. Fran and Sue were not really comfortable with this, but finally agreed we needed to get this done. Our 30-day visas expired the next day. We had to get on that boat.

Off we went. Bebang brought us to the official shipping offices where we met his friend who had his own office. He wore the uniform of the company, but he spoke no English. Bebang explained that we had to pay his friend $300 for four tickets—right now. We had to be at the bottom of the gangway at 5pm the next day to meet his friend and board. He would have our tickets and would personally present them to us then.

When we got back to the warehouse, alias hotel, we disingenuously thanked Bebang for all his help, and waved goodbye to him. The girls, in our absence, figured out that this was the equivalent of a hot sheet hotel. It was undoubtedly rented by the hour and the sheets pinned to the chain link fence were all the privacy anyone got. We came to an agreement, packed up, and marched out of the place. The guy behind the desk went ballistic. We assumed he wanted money, but he wasn't getting any from us. We pulled out the old "yellow brick road" guide-book and took a taxi to the listed youth hostel. It was cheap and good, and we slept well that night.

The next day we bought a few items for the trip back to Singapore, mostly just food to carry us. We knew what the boat was like. And we were anxious to leave. Better to be early than late, especially on the last day of a 30-day visa. We took a taxi and ran into serious traffic that ate up our early start. We crawled but made it right on time. There was a line of people boarding, and the ship officers were taking tickets at the bottom of the gangway, as we were told would happen. But we couldn't spot our guy. We then realized we didn't even know his name, but he said he'd be there. Actually, Bebang said he'd be there. He was the translator. We waited until the entire line of passengers boarded, and then tried to talk to the ship's officers to explain what we had been told. They looked at us like we were crazy, and we clearly weren't getting on the boat without tickets. We just watched as they pulled up the gangway. We weren't going anywhere. We were fools, but not just fools, we were soon to be illegal fools.

We caught a taxi back to the youth hostel. They were surprised to see us but not as surprised as we were to see them again. Fortunately, they had room. We had some things to figure out, but we had to sleep on it, and start in the morning with clear heads.

The next morning, we met and got a bite to eat as we started our day. Our first objective was to figure out what we had to do, and what we had to do first. We decided to address the visa problem first. We asked around and got directions to the American embassy. A serious building with an iron fence and gate, it gave us a strange feeling as we approached, the United States Marine guards coolly considering us. I wanted to yell "Hey we're on the same side!" They let us approach and escorted us to an office where we had a short wait with framed photos of President Ronald Reagan and Secretary of State Alexander Haig staring down at us. A staff member joined us shortly and sat at the desk in front of the two-dimensional Commander in Chief. We explained our predicament and he was sympathetic but could not offer much help. If we needed to borrow money to get home, he could do that. If we lost our passports, he could fix that. But the scam, the theft, the visa expiration, were all domestic issues and out of his hands. He offered to write, on official State Department letterhead, a summary of our problem, requesting any help that could be provided by the Indonesian officials. We welcomed that at least and thanked him. He also recommended we file a police report, just for the record, but not to expect anything from it. We left to file a report at the Jakarta police station.

The report itself was a standard questionnaire that was fed through an ancient typewriter. This took quite a while. It was a manual model with a young man who had to search for every letter he needed from the keyboard. When it was finished, the police officer who took the report just pulled it out of the machine and handed it to us. There was no carbon copy for them. They had no interest in trying to find the perps. They only responded to bribes and favors—which we didn't offer. Our man at the Embassy knew what he was talking about.

Our next stop was a large office building for immigration and border control, where we once again explained our problem. They loved the letter from the American Embassy. They passed it around and chuckled, but it didn't exactly expedite things. We filled out more forms and brought them to the office of a man who was apparently allowed to grant visa extensions. Our paperwork landed on his desk, and just stayed there. We sat politely while other people walked in and dropped their papers in front of him.

What we didn't realize at first was what was under the papers. The officer sitting at the desk used a pencil to lift up a corner, just enough, to see what was hidden by the papers that needed stamping. If he approved of what he saw, he opened his center desk drawer, and dragged the papers over it in such a way that just the money fell into it. Stamps were given all day like this. We were getting a lesson on how things worked. With each lesson he slid back and put his feet up on top of his desk and gave us a dirty grin. We wouldn't tolerate this and instead spent two days sitting there staring at him as he dragged what seemed like huge amounts of cash, into his pocket, by way of his center desk drawer. We took turns watching. There was just one of him. . . and we wore him down, sick of us! He finally stamped our papers with big bangs and tossed them in our general direction. We picked them up and left. No thanks were given.

We were free, and we would definitely make the next boat. In the meantime, what to do about Bebang Sopany. We were in a third world country where life is cheap, so we didn't want to take too many chances, especially in light of the fact that no one, including the police wanted anything to do with us.

We could have just enjoyed a little extra vacation time in Jakarta, written off the loss, *"forget about it."* But Jimi and I just couldn't let it go. We knew where he might be. We had his address, or maybe it was his uncle's address. He had led us there the day we went to meet his uncle, in a very roundabout, confusing fashion, intentionally I'm sure. We didn't really know what it was he had written for us in Fran's diary. We opened it up and were shocked to find nothing. The page had been ripped out. He must have taken it out when we were laying around on the dirty cots in the whorehouse...er hotel. He played us like a violin. That really got us. Jimi and I were fuming. Bebang was probably sitting around somewhere spending our money, knowing we wouldn't be able to find him if we tried. Maybe he thought we were even on our way to Singapore by then, having realized we had been scammed, and at the last second bought new tickets to climb the gangway and escape that lunacy. If we had had time to think, we might have done just that. But we didn't.

What Bebang didn't know was that we wrote our contacts, addresses, phone, whatever, in at least two books, one for each couple, in case we got split up somehow.

The next morning, Jimi and I took a taxi close, just short of the address we had recorded in the second book, and we recognized where we were. We walked along the open sewer toward the house we had been in. When we got close, maybe 100 feet to the door, we heard the wild screams of a young boy of about 10 who had been sitting in the window of the house we were headed to. "Bebang! . . . Bebang! . . . Bebang!" We ran toward the door but before we could get there, it opened outward with a crash and out came Bebang, running as fast as he could, up the street and away from us. There were many people in the street. Everyone turned and looked but no one moved as we yelled at the top of our lungs "Thief! Stop! Help!" Just a short way up the street, there was a corner and we didn't see which way he went, so we split up, and ran faster. Jimi then spotted him and was gaining. It was like a movie. Bebang tipped over carts of fruit, and trinkets of all kinds, more shouts, and screams, and yelling, not from Bebang, but at him for the damage he was doing to everybody and everything as he ran through the crowded street. But then he was gone.

In the meantime, I ran into a dead end. I was screaming for help as I ran up the street not knowing that Jimi almost had him. If I was the one who had taken the correct path it looked like there was only one place that could hide him. It was a dark doorway to a cement building. I ran in at full speed. It was darker inside. I yelled "Bebang!" Nothing. Then my eyes adjusted to the dark. I was exhausted, breathing heavily, and realized I was not alone. There were 12 or 13 men standing in a circle, a circle around me, but Bebang was not one of them. I yelled "Where's Bebang?" Nothing. "Bebang Sopany!" Still nothing. The thought crossed my mind that I was seriously outnumbered. I heard not a peep from even one of them. They just stared. I turned and ran through them to the bright sun and kept running, back to the uncle's, back to Jimi, where he stood waiting for me.

We knocked on the door and called out. The man we had met before, the uncle, appeared, and was obviously very confused but his English was better than we had realized. We told him everything that had happened. We told him how Bebang had lied us, had lied to his friends, had lied to his uncle. As long as Bebang controlled the conversation and the translation, as he did, he could fool everybody. We told him we were going to the police and would tell them everything, even about the uncle who sat at the table with us while Bebang plotted to scam us. He was not just confused now, but angry. Not angry with us, but with his nephew Bebang. It was possible he could lose his job at the university over something like this. He pleaded with us not to go to the police. We had forgotten to mention, luckily, that we had already been there, and they could have given a rat's ass. He asked us to wait, *"Please!"* and he re-appeared with cash in hand to make good on his nephew's theft. We said we felt so bad, he was obviously a good man. It was sad to see him stuck holding the bag. He said not to worry, he would take care of Bebang Sopany.

The next day we bought our boat tickets for the boat three days hence. They were deck passage, and cheap. We had already experienced the worst. We were veterans and would be better prepared this time.

Upon returning to the youth hostel, the young man behind the desk said that someone had been waiting for us to return. Uh-oh! He then signaled the man over from where he was sitting. He introduced himself as the director of an English language school. He asked if we were really from the United States as the desk clerk had said. We said yes and flashed our passports as proof. We conversed in English, but his own use of the language was far from perfect. He said he had booked a small class with three students for English lessons but at the last minute the teacher pulled out. When we told him we actually were teachers, he couldn't believe his good fortune. We only had three days left in Jakarta, but he said that was OK. He'd figure out what to do from there. Fran, Jimi, and I agreed to cover the three days and we would be paid $25 each. I went first. At 10 a.m. he picked me up at the hostel with his motor bike and brought me, not to a classroom, but to City Hall. Each class of conversational English lasted about an hour and a half, and it was power-packed. The first of the three students was the City Solicitor of Jakarta. Second was the Director of Finance. Third was the Director of Family Planning for the entire country. This was conversational English and I was in a position to steer where the conversation went. The school Director, sitting off to the side, became visibly ill when I ventured into the interesting topic of corruption. We learned during our short stay in Indonesia that literally everything, and everybody, in the country was corrupt. The higher the level of employment or position, public or private, the more corrupt you could be, and were expected to be. I think their whole economy depended on it. We had already seen far too many examples.

Our day of departure finally arrived. It wasn't easy, but we had made it through our 35 days in Indonesia and wondered what could possibly top that.

Kicking Back in Ko Pha Ngan

SITTING IN FRONT OF MY BLAZING WOOD STOVE, FEELING THE intensity of the fire, the heat on my face, I am reminded of a story.

We four travelers were tired. We had been on the road five (5) months and it was not what you might call 'rest and relaxation'. That's when you lay on the beach, swim or read, and someone brings you cocktails with little umbrellas.

We had started driving west from Rhode Island and after selling the car in San Francisco, we continued west by trains, planes, buses and boats through Japan, Hong Kong, mainland China, Singapore, Indonesia, and finally Malaysia, to the busy little port of Surat Thani. That's the jumping off point for the tourist islands of Koh Samui and Ko Pha Ngan, about 50 miles off the coast of southeast Thailand. Our next transportation mode was two linking ferries. We were forced to stay in Ko Pha Ngan for a week because the ferries only came by once a week. We had read about the island in our yellow guidebook, the one called the "Yellow Brick Road." The island was described as the place to 'get away from it all,' and they weren't kidding.

It was a small island with no paved roads, no restaurants, no hotels, and no electricity. We found a family that took in guests and we slept in simple thatch huts right by the sea. It was crude, but beautiful. We took all our meals with the family, and they were excellent. We didn't have anything we had to do, but we were encouraged to do lots of things.

I almost immediately started to hang around the little thatch hut that was the kitchen and I picked up a lot of cooking tips. The mother, with her young daughter, welcomed me and taught me how to do basic things like grating coconuts to make the coconut milk that served as the Thai equivalent of chicken stock, which went into practically all their dishes. It was great! We broke the language barrier with cooking and learning all the various foods.

The son in the family was very friendly and he taught me how to make a spear using a big old rusty nail and a sledgehammer. The nail was pounded into the shape of a spearhead and bound with some kind of tree fiber to a stick. Simple technology but it was something to be proud of. Not only did we make them, but we used them. Several times we went out in the night with a gas lantern and walked through knee deep water between the areas of sand and coral. There we managed to spear quite a few crabs of a kind I had never seen before. When our bucket was full, halfway through the night, we went back to the thatch hut kitchen and cooked them up by candlelight, taking turns sipping from a big bottle of Me Kong whiskey. Delicious!

One of the first mornings, the father explained to us, with difficulty, there was something on the other side of the island we should see. It was some kind of sporting event that involved chickens. We weren't sure what it was, but we didn't want to miss anything. The four of us headed a couple miles down the path as directed and finally came upon a bunch of men yelling at each other and holding fistfuls of money up in the air. When we got closer, we realized it was a cockfight. It all took place in a covered wooden structure about 25 feet in diameter. Inside was a short, circular, wooden wall; the whole thing reminded me of a miniature bull fighting arena. The actual cock fight was roosters prize-fighting with knives tied to their legs. A wind-up alarm clock, hung on a string from the ceiling, started and ended the rounds. And the fights were bloody, with all the men yelling and offering bets. These were fights to the finish. You could identify the owners and trainers of the birds. They picked them up and patched them best as possible in the couple minutes between rounds—stroking their feathers and whispering into their ears, words of encouragement I assumed. Blood poured from their head wounds and the trainers would take them aside and urinate on them. The warm sterile fluid rinsed away the blood in their eyes so they could see to fight some more. We didn't stay 'til the end. As interesting as it was, we had seen more than enough.

Ko Pha Ngan is not a big island, but it has a good mountain to climb. Round trip up and back is over two hours and the view is fantastic. It was also our good fortune to meet a Buddhist monk clothed in his saffron robe, who stayed in a small hut just below the very top of the mountain. He was an elderly gentleman who felt the call to complete his vows before he passed to the other side. He invited us to sit with him and talk. He explained his religion and he answered lots of questions. I had always wanted to ask someone like him, with a shaved head, sitting on a mountaintop, wearing a saffron robe, "What is the meaning of life?" Well, he fell a little short on that one and offered us a treat instead. He made up mugs of Chocolate Ovaltine for all of us. I asked him if this wasn't breaking his vow of not eating after midday and he said he just didn't think of it as food and shrugged it off. The Ovaltine was good! And I thought, maybe that's the meaning of life.

Another day we were having lunch and the father, once again, told us there was something else happening later that day that we should definitely see. After the chicken incident, we were a little less eager to jump into anything, but the whole family agreed we should definitely go and see this.

We weren't sure what it was, but it involved fire this time. We were told that many people would be there, especially families. Well we were game, but this time we had to stay out quite late on the other side of the island and return in the dark. This was jungle, with lots of snakes and miscellaneous creatures just waiting to attack us. And there was no moon that night. We went before sunset and did our best to memorize the route we took. It was mostly just worn paths with no markers to show the way.

We found our destination without getting lost, and it was true, there were many people—families, many young men but a majority were young women. It could have been a high school dance. The youngsters, clustered by sex were smiling, and laughing, and probably wondering what the possibilities were to be had among them. And, there was a fire. A big fire! It was a mound like a haystack, but made up of solid logs, burning themselves down to brilliant pieces of charcoal. And hot. We had worked our way to be close to the fire so we wouldn't miss "anything," whatever "anything" was going to be. The smart ones backed off a bit. There were drums. There were men dressed like witch doctors. There was one man who looked ancient and everyone recognized his status. He stood barefoot, clearly in charge of the ceremony we were there to witness.

Time passed. It was getting late. The old man came out of a small hut nearby and walked toward the fire, stopped, gave instructions, and retreated back to the hut. Two middle-aged men appeared carrying a long pole. Each held an end and used it to carefully spread the coals into an area about 20 feet by 6 feet. The coals were so hot we had to move back more to avoid the scalding heat. The fire finally settled down to about 10 inches in height, and so bright it was difficult to look into. The old man then stepped once again out of the hut but this time he had eight young men following him; they were naked to the waist and barefoot. We looked into their eyes and thought we could see the effect of drugs, or some kind of trance they were in. They moved with little steps, jumping, almost hopping to the beat of a drum, and they went around the fire, all the way around once, and then twice. Everyone watching knew what was coming and held their breath. The old man entered the fire, walking slowly through the coals, with the eight young men behind him. When he got to the end he came out and circled back to the beginning. He entered the fire again, and they all followed. It was on this second pass that one of the young men tripped and fell, pressing his entire body against the blazing coals. He tried to get up but the man behind him also tripped and knocked him completely down again. Everyone moaned but no one moved. The old man got to him and pulled him from the fire. With help, the injured young man was carried to the hut with the others, and the door was closed.

It felt like the waiting room outside the operating theater—everyone shared the pain. We waited, speaking softly to one another, for a long time. This was a "coming of age" ceremony. It was a difficult test, and not everyone passes. We almost gave up, thinking nothing but the worst...and then the door opened.

Slowly, out came the old man. Out came seven young men, and then wobbling, through the door frame, totally covered with some kind of grease that reflected the fire light, the eighth young man appeared. Everyone cheered him, but he seemed to be somewhere else in his mind, and the entourage just walked slowly into the jungle, into the darkness. And like the story of the Pied Piper, all the young women followed them into that darkness.

It was late when we started back and we had difficulty seeing after looking at nothing but the fires all evening. Our only scare was when we startled a sleeping water buffalo. We all jumped. I don't know who was more scared.

What time we had left of our seven-day island vacation was spent in honest leisure. I did a lot of cooking and I searched the beach and reef, looking for beautiful and unusual shells and rocks, finding far more than I could carry. I spent hours in a hammock, flipping the pages all the way to the end of *Atlas Shrugged*. A perfect ending all round and as good a time as any to restart our adventure north—to Bangkok.

Hiking in Northern Thailand

I COULDN'T BELIEVE THE SITUATION WE WERE IN, BUT IT WAS real, and I had to face it, and do something to help save us all. At the top of my lungs I yelled "Jimi!" and again, "Jimi!" I heard in the absolute darkness, barely audible over a symphony of jungle insects, a painful "Yaah!" I turned in the opposite direction and yelled "Franny!" Franny half answered, half screamed. "We're here, hurry!" I moved 10 or 15 paces in her direction, closer to her voice, and then turned and yelled again for Jimi. I was alone, moving toward Fran and Sue, moving away from Jimi. Splitting the distance between the two of them. Eventually, unless the guides stopped running, or Jimi got back on his feet, we would have been separated like pearls suddenly freed from a broken string. Fran and Sue did their best not to lose the trail . . . and the guides, who had panicked, and run for their own safety. We had hired them actually—a guide and a porter, both about 20 years old. Someone in Chang Rai near the border with Laos recommended them to us. But, that night, they were running scared. I wasn't afraid of the jungle, but their fear was so powerful, I believed they knew something we didn't. Like being eaten. They were deathly afraid of being eaten, and they were running for their lives, not ours. The insect noise was tremendous, but we also heard an occasional rumble that comes from deep in the lungs of big cats. This made them run faster. We stumbled against roots and vines, and rocks we could not see in the darkness. I yelled some more, for Jimi, and for Fran, and tried to stay somewhere between the two, stretching the ever-tinier vocal tether between us for as long as we could, until we could pull ourselves back together. The problem was that Jimi was ill. Ill to the point that his stomach cramps left him doubled over on the ground, relieving himself of whatever unfriendly matter he had left in his stomach and intestines. With

Jimi collapsed, and Fran trying to keep up contact with our guides, I remained the link between the two, and would, as long as I could. I didn't know what else to do. It's not something you plan.

This little adventure had started the day before. We had traveled by jeep toward the northern border of Thailand, until the road just ended. We hiked all day through amazing vegetation and were greeted by monkeys high in the tree canopy. Especially beautiful was a large area forested exclusively with very tall bamboo. A gentle breeze created gentle music from the rustle of leaves dancing high above. We walked easily. We talked. We asked questions of our guide, who spoke passable English. The porter said nothing to us. His burden was a rucksack with our food, like cooking oil, rice, noodles, and cooking pans. The food was not memorable, except perhaps in a negative way . . . just ask Jimi. . . but this trek was only 4 days. We wouldn't starve. We each carried our own water and a minimum of necessities. It was an adventure.

Late afternoon of that first day we came upon strange man-made signs of some sort, made of bamboo leaves, that hung down into the trail we were following. Our guide said they were made and placed there by the priests to ward off evil spirits. We gave them some room and only steps ahead we came upon a great opening . . . a village of thatched huts, inhabited by the hill tribe known as the 'Black Karen'. They had fled from the turmoil in the north and established their village right there. All the women wore black fabric dresses with colorful embroidery, and towels, like you might find from Walmart, wrapped around the top of their heads. I later saw several of the unveiled scalps of these women that were shaven smooth from top center forward. It seems this was a tradition started when Kublai Khan adopted the habit of invading these people's ancestors and stole the women by reaching down and pulling them up onto their horses by their hair, and just taking them home. The shaved head prevented that, just in case another Kublai Khan type were to show up again.

Luckily for us, we arrived just in time for great celebrations—the opium harvest. This was, after all, part of the famous opium triangle.

We went out into the fields of white poppies and were shown how to slit the base of the white poppy flowers so the rubbery sap could ooze out and be collected later in the day.

When we got back to the center of the village, we followed squeals to a restrained pig and watched as a tribesman slit its throat and drained the pulsing blood into a pan, undoubtedly for some kind of specialty food. A fire had already been started—green logs laid across the top of a hot fire to lay the pig upon in order to scrape the coarse hair from its body as it burned free. They slit the pig and gutted it to the amusement of all the naked children running around it. One of the organs, the bladder I believe, became a balloon—blown up, tied off and tossed to the kids who carried it off to play a kind of ball game. How much fun is that? We strolled back to the center and found a nonstop band, with string instruments, and dancers that would stay dancing for three days. Everyone was friendly, but it seemed they might have thought we were a bunch of not so bright weirdos. One little towel-headed girl of about eight or nine got into a staring contest with me and she ended up winning by flicking the cigarette she was smoking at my face, so I jumped back of course. This little kid smoking was the cause of my staring in the first place. These people were tough.

This was a small village of 50 or so. There was no plumbing. There was a stream. There were no bathrooms, or outhouses— just poppy fields and jungle around us. There were also dogs, and pigs—a number of pigs, who in my opinion are far more intelligent than they are given credit for. If someone stepped into the jungle to do what we used to call #1. . . no big deal. The pigs couldn't care less. You did number 1. If you were aiming at a #2, you didn't make it more than a few steps toward the jungle before you had all the pigs excitedly gathered around you in anticipation. They were all excited . . . you couldn't do it. Stupid foreigners. We were laughingly shown the stick that leaned up against each of the thatch dwellings, for the purpose of beating off the pigs until you were done. When you were done, you jumped up, quickly out of the way, as they charged and devoured every bit with relish. . . especially the paper. Mind you, we were eating one of these creatures at the big opium harvest celebration that very night.

When it was dark, we sat in on the dancing, and a bit of the food, and the music, so unusual and rhythmic, I thought I would never forget it. We also got a chance to sample this year's harvest. We each took a turn laying down on the floor of a hut, with a small lamp burning nearby. The headman of the hut we were in took a pea-sized ball of poppy resin and mixed it with a little aspirin powder and massaged it with his thumb in the palm of his hand. He then pressed it onto a small hole on the side of a short stick of bamboo. He pierced that with a pin that could have been made from a paper clip. One at a time, we laid down on our sides, our heads supported by a pillow. We inhaled deeply, gently drawing a small flame from the oil lamp, through the bamboo and into the resin until it bubbled up and smoked. We drew the smoke into our lungs until the resin had entirely bubbled away. ZOWIE! It was a good thing you couldn't get this at home. We all tried it and we noticed that our guide and our porter were already experts.

The next morning, we were up and ready to hike to the second of our hill tribe villages when we realized two of us were missing, namely our guide and our porter. We didn't remember the end of the evening and didn't know where to look for them. When they finally showed, it was late. Seriously late. Only they knew how serious it was. We had quite a distance to hike to the next Hmong village. No stopping now just moving quickly. No leisurely stroll now . . . hurry! And this is how we found ourselves, in the jungle, in total darkness, accompanied by the never-ending symphony of insects, and an occasional rumble from deep in the lungs of a big cat that seemed to be following us.

Jimi finally got up and struggled toward my voice. I struggled toward Fran's. Fran chased Sue's voice, and, little by little we compressed our accordion, until we found ourselves rejoined, in total darkness, nearly lost. We couldn't find the trail anymore; even the guides had stopped because they didn't know which way to run. We fished a can of cooking oil from the porter's rucksack. Jimi skimmed off his already badly soiled t-shirt, wrapped and tied it to a stick and soaked it in the oil. When it lit it was bright, but the path was not clear, so we walked in the shallow water of the fortunately sluggish Mei Kong river to keep our direction correct. We followed it with its ups and downs, holes and boulders and other surprise obstacles and finally, we arrived on a bank where torches were lit to guide us in. More thatched huts. We ate a little food. We had arrived, but we were sore and scratched, exhausted, and wet, and soon passed to sleep on woven straw mats, surrounded by the sounds and the darkness of the jungle.

Sometime later in the night, we were poked awake, and forced to move so our bodies faced in the proper direction so the gods would not be angry. They told us if they had let us sleep, they would have had to break down the village and move the entire group of thatched huts to somewhere else. We would have caused it unknowingly, by our ignorant, inconsiderate sleeping habits.

We woke tired, but there was not the hurry of the previous day. The jungle by day, in the sunlight, was warm and welcoming. The few inhabitants of this Hmong tribe were hardly noticing us, and that was fine. I'm sure our guide paid everyone a few baht for accommodating us. We left for the next and last hill tribe and arrived easily before dark. Our beds were like bunks, over a dirt floor inside a thatched hut. We stayed here with a family. It was good. We sang, we ate, the children giggled . . . we tried on each other's clothes . . . it was fun.

When we woke in the morning it was to a gunshot. The father and head of the family stood proudly framed in the doorway, with his ancient flintlock rifle, and showed us his trophy, already cleaned and stretched across some sticks, ready for the cook fire. I had never eaten squirrel . . . and still haven't. Fortunately, maybe, we ate what was left of our own food instead, even though this family was quite willing to share their meager rations.

After heartfelt goodbyes and rigorous waving, we departed and followed our guide, and porter back to a rendezvous where a jeep was waiting. Our thoughts were already getting ahead of us. We quickly retrieved our stored gear in Chang Rei, and caught an overnight bus to Bangkok, in time for our next flight . . . to Kathmandu, Nepal.

I wouldn't recommend our guide and porter, but they certainly knew how to enhance an adventure.

The Storyteller

It was back in 1981. There were four of us, two young couples, with a year off, traveling around the world. We gained entrance into China by using forged documents obtained from a man living in Hong Kong that we had heard about all the way back in Kyoto, Japan. Getting into China was one thing but getting out again might have been another. We were very foolish to take the chance and found that even being there as tourists fell into that "difficult" category. Prices were not the problem. Everything was so cheap that someone could have written a book, "China on $5 a Week". The problem was that there was no tourism, or any systems yet in place for travelers to eat, sleep, or meander within the huge country. It had been closed to the outside world for decades and had only recently showed signs of opening up the "Red Curtain" by letting Nixon and Kissinger slip through. English speakers were few and far between. In one large city, Wuhan, we actually looked all day for a hotel or any place just to crash that night. The only thing we found was an opium den, with what looked like bunk beds, wooden racks really, that already held a number of patrons. Some of them were out cold, a few of them were awake in the dim afternoon light, with glazed, unseeing, uncaring eyes. We couldn't do it. Instead, desperate, we coerced passage on a boat late that night going down the Yangtze. China was very difficult, but we were rewarded with incredible experiences that turned into incredible memories. We were foreigners. We were objects of fascination. If we stopped moving anywhere as we walked the cities, especially the smaller ones, crowds would form around us and stare, and point, and sometimes delicately reach out and touch our bare arms, just to feel the hairs. They were like little children, we were like harmless animals in a petting zoo. So strange were we that

Chinese mothers and fathers would hold up small children above the heads of others that they might see too, and catch a glimpse of we strange Caucasians, the likes of which they had never seen before.

It was almost Thanksgiving Day back home, on the other side of the planet. The weather was cool, rainy, gentle but steady. I remember walking all around the large city of Nanjing. It was not a tall city. There were no skyscrapers, just street after street, pedestrians and push carts, sandwiched between the short cement buildings turned sooty dark from everyone burning coal. Also attributed to the coal smoke: hacking and coughing and spitting—everywhere—in the streets, and all public places like restaurants and train stations, inside or out. You heard and saw the coughing up of phlegm, which they spit with gusto, without a thought. Walking was slippery and dangerous.

Everything in China looked dim and gloomy, partly from the coal, and we were just miserable walking around in the rain, hoping to find a place to have a special Thanksgiving meal. We didn't expect anyone in China knew about this, but we were determined to give it the old college try and see what we could find for a feast, just for the four us.

After walking around for a good part of the day, we came upon a place that had possibilities. It was a fairly new-looking cement structure about the size of an American one car garage. There were a few round tables and chairs, just waiting for business. We entered and introduced ourselves to a man standing by the door, one of two persons on the premises. We took him to be either the manager, or owner. We explained to him what we had in mind, which was a Thanksgiving banquet, the very next day, for the four of us. Then we invited ourselves into the kitchen and explained to the chef (at least we thought he was the chef) what we wanted to eat. . . which was a little of everything. Of course, not one word we said, or they said, was understood even a little by us or them. Even imitations of all the barnyard animals we wanted to eat might have fallen a little short, but we figured at least some of it would sink in. And we all had a good laugh in the kitchen mooing, cock-a-doodle-doing, and quacking, some other possibilities. Who doesn't like Thanksgiving?

We all shook hands, "until tomorrow," and back we slipped into the light rain. We saw some shelter and ducked under the pediments of the famous Yangtse River Bridge. The bridge was built at this spot as a tribute to Mao Tse-tung. This is where, as a young revolutionary he swam across the Yangtse River and added to his growing fame. It is particularly wide there and the dark waters run swift as they make their way east to Shanghai, and on into the South China Sea. There we were, running and taking cover from a burst of rain, under the base of the bridge, between giant cement pediments that raised the road before it crossed from shore to shore. We were not alone. . . far from it. We found ourselves in the presence of perhaps 50 or 60 Chinese, all sitting on stumps and stones that lay scattered on the riverbank, under cover of the bridge above. They sat facing down the bank toward a giant concrete wall, almost at the water's edge. They were dressed like the rest of China that we saw, males and females the same. Mao suits we called them. They came in any color you wanted, as long as you wanted green or blue, with matching hats. Some had plastic stars pinned above the brims, that indicated past military service. All of the Chinese were smoking, nonstop, cigarette after cigarette. The smoke blended with the moist air. You could tell the tobacco was rough, but cheap enough for even the poorest comrades to steadily puff away. Inside buildings the smoke could be unbearable. We were out in the air, cold and damp, but at least we could breathe. Due to the overcast sky, and being under the bridge, it was fairly dark. When our eyes adjusted, we discovered we had stumbled into not just a place to take shelter, but into the realm of a storyteller, facing his audience and gathering attention with his eyes. He was a small old Chinese man with a thin scraggly beard, also garbed in a Mao suit that had obviously seen many years, perhaps decades in Red China. Oh to be a fly on the wall, or a suit on a man, during the turmoil of the Cultural Revolution and the Great Leap Forward. He sat upon a well-worn stump that looked like it had been polished by many a posterior. We decided to stay and watch and found places to sit up behind the audience so we wouldn't be obvious. When the old man started, all sat rapt as they listened to the singsong Chinese of the storyteller. With starry eyes that penetrated the gloom, he held the audience in the palm of his hand. Of course, we understood not one word of the story, but it was enough just to observe the master. He had an old string instrument of some kind that looked like half of a homemade violin. He held it in his lap with one hand and from time to time for the emphasis of some point he was trying to make, he would grab a string with his free hand and give it a loud plink! This helped keep attention high. Another technique he used effectively was silence. For short periods the audience would hang, motionless, with only the sound of rain, and the distant muffled noise from the occasional truck as it passed on the bridge somewhere above us. And that's how it went, for some time, drawn in as we were to the rhythm, and melody and comfortable song of the old man's story.

Then, with one particularly loud and abrupt phrase, the storyteller stopped, plinked, and all was silent. Each and every man and woman under that bridge turned on their rocks and stumps to look back, back at the strange Caucasians directly behind them. Staring with glaring suspicion, and no one returned our smiles. We froze. We did not know the story, but we knew, for better or worse, we had become part of it. After a pause that seemed endless, the storyteller turned everyone around again, continued on and brought about a conclusion that appeared to satisfy everybody, and we were okay. A small crude basket was passed and a few coins, renminbi, collected. I would love to know what he said about us but maybe, some stories, with their endings, are better left to the imagination.

The next day we returned to our restaurant for our Thanksgiving feast where we thought we had reservations. The same gentleman was there but when he saw us it was like seeing us for the first time. The restaurant was as empty as it had been the day before. We just went in and sat down. Then we started making gestures like eating and they finally got the point and started to prepare we knew not what but right from the start, it was good. As soon as we almost finished a bowl or plate, we made more gestures and a few minutes later out of the kitchen came another dish of some kind. Our chopsticks got quite a workout.

News on the street was that four foreigners were in the restaurant, eating like crazy, everything as fast as they could cook it. It started with lots of locals staring through the open windows in wonder. Then they filled the area around our table, watched over our shoulders and made comments and exclamations to each other about us, the food, our ability to eat so much, and probably, our ability to pay for it. There were smiles on all the faces. We offered the bits of leftovers we just couldn't finish, and we were all loving the company. The manager cleared all the plates from the table and returned with four bowls with a clear hot liquid. We stared and smelled, wondering what this was until finally one of the men around us reached over our shoulders and dunked his hands in. Finger bowl . . . elegant, top shelf. Everyone cheered!

The Real China

CHINA. IT WAS A GREAT TRIP. NEARLY 40 YEARS AGO. AND STILL every time I go to my local Chinese restaurant, I think of it. It brings back memories.

In 1981, myself, my new wife Susan, and our best friends Fran and Jimi took a year off to circle the planet. We roughly planned our itinerary, wanting to visit all the exotic ports of call we could squeeze into a year. One we didn't list was mainland China. It wasn't open. Even nine years after Nixon's historic visit, westerners could not travel to China on their own. They had to be part of an official, licensed, tourist group. Or so we thought.

But in Kyoto Japan, outside one of the famous Buddhist temples, I met a young lady, whose name I no longer remember. I do remember her smile, and long hair and dress. She was sort of a late-20-something free-spirited hippie. Her sandals, along with our sneakers, lay among the vast collection of shoes left outside by all those entering the temple. She was a fellow circumnavigator, but seeing the world in the opposite direction, west to east, not traveling west like us. We compared notes and she mentioned China as her favorite thus far and said, "You are we planning to go, aren't you?" Yes of course, we were in fact flying to Hong Kong when we left Japan. She said, "I don't mean Hong Kong, I mean mainland China, the real China." This took us by surprise because we didn't think it was possible. She assured us it was in fact and told us how to do it.

That's how we found ourselves some two weeks later on the 16th floor of the Chun King Mansion in the center of Kowloon, Hong Kong. It was a big office building, twisted with corridors and stairwells to nowhere. It was full of traders with various costumes from all over the world. I remember the heat, incense-like fragrances, body odors resulting from the sweltering heat of Hong Kong, and busy sounds and many languages, especially of south-east Asia and the Middle East.

We asked about and found the man we were told to look for. He stood behind an empty podium in the hallway. This served, in his few square feet, as his desk, and his entire office. His name was Lee, like so many others there and that was all we had. But when we approached him there was no question. He looked at us. We looked at him. "We heard you might be able to help us get into mainland China." Without even hello and after only a moment's hesitation he looked at us and said, "Give me your passports, and $30 each."

"Whoa!" We guarded our passports and had them tucked safely into pouches hung around our necks under our shirts and acted as if everyone wanted to steal them and make life very difficult for us. But we reflected just a moment and handed them over. He pocketed everything, said "Come back in three days", and disappeared down the hall through a cast of world characters. For better or worse, the die was cast.

The next three days we saw Hong Kong and returned each evening to another office building we had heard about. Offices of some sort by day, flop house by night where for two dollars you could claim a sleeping bag-sized piece of carpet, all your own. Word had gotten around and about 25 backpacker-types crowded the floor each night. One discomfort was the fluorescent lighting that never turned off. Also, we had to be gone before the first office employees entered in the morning. But it was cheap! We decided to celebrate one of the evenings of humid heat with cold beers. Fran and I volunteered to find our way out of the building with twists and turns as Sue and Jimi held the fort and our claims to pieces of carpet. It took us maybe two hours, but we found cold beers and finally found our way back through the fire trap we called home. When Sue saw us and the beers, she said "Where the hell did you go for the beers. . . China?"

When we returned to find Lee three days later, he was still standing in the same place. Without a word, he handed us our passports with official looking stamps and a full page of Chinese characters that could have been a grocery list, for all we knew.

The next morning, we rode an old British train through the New Territories to the end of the line. From there we followed the railroad tracks and a small file of Chinese to a railroad trestle, that crossed a deep ravine maybe 200 feet wide. On the other side was mainland China, the real China, and a barrier of Chinese soldiers with rifles held across their chests, staring across at us. We walked forward, carefully stepping on each tie so as not to fall into the ravine below. They watched us come. They looked nervous. When we got to the other side and just feet from the soldiers, they blinked—and parted like the Red Sea. We walked through them and kept walking, not looking back until we came to a waiting train. We somehow bought tickets and boarded just in time to continue on to Guangzhou, formerly known as Canton. We arrived there late, and tired, and hungry. We found a dormitory to house us for the night and then went in search of food. We found only one place open where we might eat. It was a special restaurant and the only item served was dog.

Sometimes now, when I am hungry and don't feel like cooking, I go to my local Chinese restaurant where I can order food at the bar and have an exotic drink with a little umbrella in it. I got to know the bartender a little. She calls herself Judy but of course that's not her real name. Other patrons, almost always men, sit at the bar and do the same thing I do.

One night it was unusually slow and for the first time I was able to talk to Judy for any length of time. I asked, "Where are you from?"

She said, "I from China."

I said, "I know you are from China but what part?"

She asked, "You know China?"

"Yes, a little bit."

Judy said "I from Canton. You know Canton?"

"Yes, a little. Guangzhou."

"Waa" she said, "You do know China."

"Yes a little."

"You like China? You like Guangzhou?"

"Yes."

"What you like in Guangzhou?"

I said, "I liked the people, and the food I remember, is very good."

"What food you remember?

I said, "I remember my first meal in China. It was dog."

It was like I dropped a bomb. She was silent. She said nothing and then: "You like dog?"

I said "It was unusual, but good. Do you like dog?"

She stopped and looked both ways down the bar to see if anyone was listening—and then said, trembling a bit, "I wuv dog!"

I nodded slowly with a smile and without missing a beat I asked, "Do you like cat?" I was going out on a limb about this. I didn't know if they ate cats in Guangzhou. But Judy answered, "I WUV cat!"

I still go to that Chinese restaurant from time to time. It reminds me of that big trip nearly forty years ago. And I do love those little umbrella drinks. Sometimes I see Judy and we're friendly, but I know she is thankful that I don't bring up that day when her culinary enthusiasms carried her best judgement away, and maybe put her job at risk. After all, her boss might not have appreciated her open honesty quite as much as I certainly did.

Sweet Potato Queens

I WAS IN THE TOWN OF SAN MIGUEL DE ALLENDE, IN THE STATE of Guanajuato, in the middle of Mexico. My former wife and I had spent a lot of time there over the years. We had lots of good times, and good friends but this was my first trip back, alone, and it took just a few days to realize I needed to break out, do something new in a new place.

I packed my things, left my little casita, and walked to the center of town where I knew of a travel agency. I told them I wanted to go somewhere. They asked where, and I said I didn't know, but I pointed to my bag by the door, and said I was ready. Only minutes later I was in a speeding taxi that I had hailed from the front of the agency. The driver, energized by the promise of a good tip, got to Leon on time for me to catch a flight to Mexico City, with a connection to Oaxaca, in southern Mexico. Something new, something different.

I waited for the connecting flight from Mexico City along with the other passengers. They were the usual mix. Some businessmen, tourists, families, all kinds. One woman did stand out because she was pretty, very well-dressed, with care in her make-up, hair, and just the right jewelry. We obviously lived in two different worlds.

Well I'm sure everyone sized everyone else up, and then we just waited for the plane to load. It was then that I noticed an older man who struggled a bit in his plastic chair to come to a stand, before heading toward the men's room. I hesitated just a second but thought "Let me see if he needs help." I came to his side, and he took my arm and leaned on me to steady himself as I guided him through the waiting area. I waited by the men's room door and again, steadied him all the way back to his seat. It was a small thing. He thanked me and I returned to my seat to wait.

When we finally boarded and found our seats for the one-hour flight to Oaxaca, I found myself just an arm's reach across the aisle from the very pretty, well-dressed woman I had spotted in the waiting area. I noted a hint of a lovely delicate perfume and added this to her persona. After buckling up we both happened to catch each other's glance and smiled and said "Hi." There was a little small talk. She was from Kentucky. She was meeting a girlfriend already staying in a small hotel in the center of town. She told me her name was Leslie. She knew where she was going. I had no clue. But I knew I had to get to town so I suggested we share a taxi to save a little money, and I would just figure what I was doing from there. She told me that she doesn't normally talk to strangers like she was doing, but she had a good safe feeling about me. She said it was a wonderful thing I did helping that old gentleman get to the rest room.

When we arrived at the airport in Oaxaca, it was a confusing scene of people and luggage. I travel light, so I helped her with bags. We had a nice ride to the small hotel, and I helped her into the reception area. I didn't have a place to stay, so I asked about rooms and rates, and although it was a little more than I wanted to spend, it was getting late and it would be dark soon making it difficult to navigate with my gear around the strange new town, searching for cheaper digs.

After checking in and getting settled, I knocked at Leslie's room and she seemed pleasantly surprised. Then I met her girlfriend Chrissie, from Texas. Leslie had already told her about this guy she had met and I knew I was getting a once over. I asked if anyone was as hungry as I was, and off we three went to find a restaurant. When we sat down in a nice little place in the central plaza, I scanned the menu, and said, "Wow, they have an appetizer of fried grasshoppers." I kidded and asked, "Anyone interested?" To my surprise, they both chirped "Yeah, let's split an order." And that was how it started. The next three days we chummed around, like tourists should, and saw and did everything that colorful Oaxaca had to offer.

Unfortunately, for me, I was really blowing my budget. I made a decision. I had to get out of town to somewhere I could exist a little more modestly, but still have a good time. The three of us sadly walked to the bus station that evening to buy me the ticket that would be splitting us up. I was going to Puerto Escondido, a beach on the Pacific, with thatch huts, big surf, and fresh seafood. My two new friends waited for me as I slowly progressed in the long line at the window to buy my ticket for the following day. I had just one more person in front of me when the two girls ran up excitedly and said they had been talking to some people that had been to Chiapas and that it sounded wonderful and exciting and they were thinking that they would love to go but that it wasn't safe for women traveling there alone, but if I would go with them it would be alright and they would be very careful with money and we could split the cost of one big room together and it would be great if I thought so too . . . I was next up at the window and when I got there I said "tres boletos para San Cristobal de las Casas, Chiapas. Por favor." That's three tickets to Chiapas, please!

Now this had already been an adventure, and we had two more weeks together. The next day we boarded a bus. We established a cash kitty, and I was given the responsibility to keep it straight. At the end of each day, as we stretched all three across the one big bed in our shared room, I gave them an account from my little notebook, how much we spent, where it had gone to, and how much we had to contribute to make the kitty whole for the following day. I enjoyed this. And it was working I thought.

But several days into our economy travel, I was approached by Chrissie, while Leslie was in the shower. She said, "Allan, I just want to tell you how much fun we're havin', and how well you are handling our money. You are doin' a wonderful job, but. . . I just wanted to tell you, you don't have to be quite so careful with our money. We don't need to know where every centavo goes . . . let me give you one little bitty example of what I mean. Leslie there, her ex-husband invented (insert world-famous household product here), she has three children, and when each turned 21, they received thirty million dollars . . . so

I'm just sayin' ya don't have to be quite so careful with our money . . . if you know what I mean....and please don't say anything to Leslie about this." Okay!

Hmmmm . . . Wow!

The next day, when Chrissie was off somewhere by herself, Leslie approached me and said I was doing a wonderful job handling their money, but I didn't have to be so careful. For example, Chrissie's daddy, as a young man had managed to buy most of the oil rights in Texas . . . .and Chrissie still owned them. And please, don't tell Chrissie I said anything. Okay!

My two friends were among the wealthiest of the wealthy. But we got along very well. And they were enjoying our frugal but exciting journey together. They called themselves a couple "Sweet Potato Queens" making a bit of fun about themselves.

San Cristobal de las Casas, the modern and historical center of the region served as our new home base for adventure. We traveled around a lot by bus. We spent a few days on the Guatemalan border with a tribe of Indians, the Lacandones, who wore what looked like white bed sheets as their only clothing, and spoke little Spanish, mostly their local indigenous tongue with lots of hand signs. We toured the ruins of Palenque for a couple days and it was there we ran into our first Howler monkeys, roaring like lions, that scared the daylights out of us. We swam and bathed in waterfalls and hot springs.

We dallied for a day in San Juan de Chamula. I don't do cathedrals anymore, having had my fill a long time ago—with this one exception. You leave the bright sunshine and enter darkness, there being no windows, only small holes in the ceiling that created shafts of light filled with dust and incense. On the floor are hundreds of small candles stuck with melted wax between fragrant fresh cut pine boughs, and there are lots and lots of people—shamans and sorcerers, the disfigured, the crippled, the blind, the insane, the possessed, and chickens everywhere, cackling with tied feet, whose blood was freely spilled to the stone floor as offerings for healing.

We shared all these things.

And, near the end of our trip together, stretched out once again across a big bed, I gave them a final brief report on our shared finances. After all I still had to watch my money. It was then, we all agreed on two things—friendship forever, and that this was the best vacation, at any cost, each of us had ever had.

Tango in Grand Rapids

Up until a few years ago, when I retired, I was an active member of the International Plant Propagators Society. Every two years, plant propagators from around the world converged and shared the latest in propagation techniques, and the business of plants, in general. One year the conference was in Grand Rapids, Michigan. My flight was uneventful except for my conversation with my cheap seats companion. Fortunately he was a very interesting old guy and an exceptional conversationalist, to say the least. He gave me his life story, as I gave him mine. We both learned a lot and our flight ended way before we would have been finished talking.

There were two topics I remember best. The first was dry cleaning. He owned several stores, sort of a king in the dry-cleaning world of the greater Boston area. Go ahead, ask me anything about dry cleaning, from the chemicals, to handling the toughest spots, and I probably learned the answer. Fascinating stuff! And he spoke with an accent. I'm usually pretty good at guessing countries of origin, but this was a tough one. I finally gave up and politely just asked him. I do this all the time. It's like a game. I usually say something like "Excuse me but I hear the tiniest bit of foreign accent in your voice . . . am I correct?" I say the same thing if I can barely understand them at all . . . just to help them believe their English is almost perfect and encourage them to even more interesting conversation. His accent brought about a second best-remembered topic of conversation that day, and brought him back to his youth, parents, grandparents, and their history that he carried throughout his life.

His ancestors were Armenian. They were victims of great atrocities in Armenia. and it was called by many "The Great Armenian Genocide." Millions were killed. His parents and grandparents fled.

Struggling across what was then Armenia, across Turkey, and Greece, from where they were able to escape by boat to Italy, and eventually to France. His memories of childhood were growing up in Marseille, France, under World War II German occupation. I asked him what that was like. He said, "To me it was just normal." The Germans were human beings, and for the most part didn't create hardship for he and his family. He conjured up images of soldiers passing out candy bars to the kids, and cigarettes to their parents. He couldn't say it was a different experience, because he had only one. When the war ended, the candy bars switched from German chocolates to Hershey bars. The most powerful memories he did have were of the holocaust. The Armenian Holocaust, that his family lived through and escaped from.

They passed down the memories, the atrocities of 1913 and '14 and made him feel like he was there —and would never forget. Until that day, on that plane, I knew nothing about the "other genocide,", as he called it. A truly interesting and educational flight. And my day was just beginning.

Back then, I was very much into dancing: the tango, to be exact. I had learned the basics on a trip to Buenos Aires, where it all started. Whenever I went anywhere, I would look to the internet to see if there were dancing opportunities of which I might take advantage. Tango dancers are everywhere. Tango dancers are like no other, serious, skillful, and artistic. To tango in a new city brought differences and similarities to view . . . yes, tango dancers are like no others. And luck was with me. There was a dance (called a milonga) happening that very night, just a few blocks away from my hotel.

I dressed and walked to the address and was greeted at the door where I paid a modest entrance fee. It was a small but comfortable venue that held perhaps 50 or 60 people. The music and dancing had already started so I found a place to sit and watch a bit before I tried to find a dance partner. I changed into my tango shoes. Everyone was dressed in the tango style—high heeled shoes, artsy flowing fabrics that opened and closed with the turns and swirls, and jewelry and hair styles that could be right out of an Argentinian fashion magazine. I was a stranger to this group and felt the stares on the back of my neck. I guess they weren't used to people dropping in from out of the blue as I did. The dancers were different, interesting, and talented, and enjoying themselves. They mostly danced with the same partners again and again, and I tried to note who was with who. I didn't want to become an intrusion of any kind.

I noticed one young woman who was especially well dressed, and very beautiful, with an olive complexion and a silver comb nestled in rich mahogany hair. She sat with several other ladies at a table on the opposite side of the room. I didn't want to stare, as staring can be dangerous unless one is very careful. If I stared at her, and caught her eye, I would be obligated to dance with her, if she wished it so—and I wasn't ready yet. I watched her as, several times, she appeared to turn down dance invitations. When someone would try to engage her by eye contact, she turned away, and in effect said "no." I was surprised to see this. She was at a dance, but thus far had yet to dance with anyone. But she was beautiful, and I stared, and caught her eye. She hesitated just a moment and gave me the slightest of nods. I stood, crossed the room, gave her my hand, and escorted her to the dance floor.

As was custom, we didn't say a word. We took a dance position. She closed her eyes, and when the music started, I lead us to the beat, rocking slightly to synchronize our feet—and then we stepped off. I could feel the stares of the entire room, but I didn't notice whether it was I, or the beautiful woman that I danced with, that was the recipient of those stares. But we gave them a show, dancing three times, which was proper.

I escorted her back to her table with her three companions, and Elana—she finally introduced herself to me as I did to her— asked me if I cared to join them. I was quite happy to do so. We chatted a bit and I finally asked her why she danced with me, after she clearly had turned down numerous opportunities with other anxious young men in the room. It seems she knew all of the men, and simply put, thought they were ignorant. . . stupid. . . and she just wanted nothing to do with them. I was taken aback, struck silent, wondering what she could mean by this. She went on "For example, I am Armenian. These people know nothing about me or what being an Armenian means. They are stupid!" I didn't know what to say. But she stopped, and stared at me, and hesitantly, asked "Are you like them? Do you know anything about my country, Armenia, my people, our struggle?" I couldn't believe my ears. I didn't know what I should say.

What I did say was "Do you mean the Armenian genocide of 1913 and '14?" Millions dying. The mass exodus of Armenians forced from their homeland, across the length of Turkey and through Greece and finally to the relative safety of Italy and France? She sat frozen to her chair. Unflinching for a few moments, until a gentle smile moved across her beautiful face. She leaned slowly forward, staring into my eyes, and just inches from my ear, gently whispered "Let's dance!" and we did, until the wee hours of the morning.

Her Name was Ungi

I HAVE ALWAYS LOVED TO EAT AND COOK. I REMEMBER AS A LIT-
tle boy hardly old enough to see the top of the kitchen stove, making
scrambled eggs with fried onions. It was simple, of course, but I liked
it and I liked cooking it for others to enjoy. Sometimes I would cook
outside on a stove I had fashioned out of a Hawaiian Punch can—
one end cut out and with air vents cut in the side, sitting upside down
over a smaller bean-sized can filled with wax and cardboard. It made
a great stove and when the first thing you cooked was Jiffy Pop, you
had an empty frying pan ready for the next course—like fried Spam
and beans. I slowly, over the years worked my way up and reached a
personal pinnacle when I was summoned from the kitchen by one of
my wait staff from the dining room of the country inn that I owned.
As I left the fluorescent lights of the kitchen and pushed through the
swinging doors into the dining room wondering what the problem
could be, my eyes adjusted to the dim light of the many candles on
the tables of the 50-plus guests. Then I realized they were all standing
by their seats, and they broke into serious applause, just for me. I had
come a long way since scrambled eggs and onions. But, as an old, wise
man once told me, "When you think you are on top of the world, the
only way to go is down."

But that's not what I'm here to tell you about. It's more of a story
like the old detectives in the 1950's. How they often started off . . .

Her name was Ungi. She was half Japanese, half Korean, and a
dish all the way. I first discovered her as she leaned way over a pool
table, one leg sort of off the floor and hiked up a bit to make a difficult
shot. She wore a short skirt but was careful not to be too provocative
as she mounted the table. It didn't work. I knew right then I was in

trouble. She had the delicate features of a porcelain doll, but she also curved in all the right ways.

I don't know what it is about attraction and how it works, but I do know there is a certain excitement that comes from something new and different. Imagination plays a part I'm sure and I imagined what it would be like to speak with her, to touch her, to be touched by her in a familiar way. I had to meet her.

She played her game quite well and quickly disposed of her young male opponent. He didn't seem to mind and for her part, she expected nothing less from herself. It was her way.

I watched her intently, as inconspicuously as I could. I dared not get too close to reveal myself too soon, and crash land before I could plan a strategy. And, I certainly didn't want to end up in a pool game which I knew would be a quick end of me.

Ungi hadn't even noticed me, but I watched every move she made. Her hair was long and straight. Her skin was a very light olive-tone and highlighted by just a touch of color at her lips and eyes. I wondered about her fragrance. I listened closely to her voice as she called her shots, thick with an Asian accent, a bit musical, but staccato-like. Difficult to understand unless you could see what she was doing. But all that seemed to enhance the attraction—something new and different.

I just wanted to meet her and would make myself satisfied by that alone if it should come to pass.

I was sitting at the bar. There weren't too many people there on that weeknight. I had been on my way home after work when something moved me to stop by, for just one beer and although I drank slowly, I was then on my second and didn't want to leave yet. It was then that she unexpectedly, with small quick steps, walked up to the bar, stood in the empty spot beside me and ordered a beer for herself.

I rolled the dice and said "Hi" She turned her head and decided to answer me with "Hi" heavy with accent. We started small talking and I sort of guessed what she was saying, not wanting to embarrass her by drawing attention to her difficult speech. I think she was used to it. I volunteered little about myself but asked her many questions about her path to this night, to this bar. We exchanged names and I immediately forgot hers . . . it seemed so foreign. I asked her to write it for me and I think I still have that bar napkin somewhere. And oh, she did have a scent, and whether applied or natural, it was most pleasant.

She was born in Korea. Her father was Japanese. She had married and divorced an American sailor. She was for all intents and purposes an American citizen, alive and well. But she referred to Korea as "her country" several times. I asked her about the things she missed from growing up there and there were many, but the food she missed caught my ear. After all, I have always loved to eat and cook.

I asked Ungi particulars about which Korean foods she most loved and missed. I didn't recognize much from the list, but I knew I would soon learn more. She, for some reason, had never learned to cook. Since living in this country, she ate to live. I lived to eat.

We finally rose from our stools and agreed to look forward to bumping into each other again sometime . . . and she left a trail for me to follow, of her favorite spots and days.

I had done it. I met her. I talked to her for maybe an hour. I should have been satisfied with that, but my imagination was still active. I wanted to learn more about. . . . Korean food!

Ungi had mentioned that a popular snack served at the bars in Korea was fried grasshoppers. She loved them with their delicate crunch and salty taste that went so well with beer. No wonder they served them—sort of like pretzels, or those fish crackers they serve to get you to drink more. I just happened to have a farm and I was plagued like never before, or since, with grasshoppers. What could be more perfect? I did a little research, but information was sparse in those days before the internet. I was always improvising recipes anyway so I just figured I'd give it a try and how difficult could it be frying grasshoppers?

Following the trail she had left me I ran into Ungi. She was even prettier than I remembered. We soon took up where we left off, back at the bar. I still had trouble with her accent, but I tried hard to understand. I announced to her that I had taken a sudden interest in Korean food and would like to cook for her, one of her favorites. She was a little surprised but accepted my invitation to dinner at my house the following week. This just seemed too good to be true.

As all good cooks know, preparation is nine-tenths of the battle. In my case, I started off, not in the kitchen, but at my farm. With a white plastic gallon milk jug, I started collecting dinner, or at least the appetizer. I learned how to spot them, sneak up on them, and pounce quickly before they jumped and flew away. I caught them one at a time and it is amazing how many it takes to fill even part of a gallon jug. As I caught each one, I quickly lifted the cap and pushed it head-first inside. They were very excited these grasshoppers. The noise alone as they crashed into the walls of the jug made you feel a little bad for them—sort of like putting lobsters in boiling water.

I lost count of how many I had captured, but I had a lot. The next part of the preparation was easy—just freeze them, bottle and all.

Although I don't remember what else I cooked that evening, it was quite a night. She was beautiful. We were in no hurry to eat. We listened to music and chatted as we sat on my couch. We had beers, her favorite, and it became time to prepare the hot appetizer. As I mentioned, Ungi was more the appreciator of food rather than the cook, so she stood back and observed in my small but well-equipped kitchen. Here was the plan: First, in my largest fry pan an inch or so of peanut oil was brought to a high temperature but not quite to the point of smoking. Most other oils, especially the fruity oils like olive oil, burn easily, destroying the nutrition of the oil and the flavor of the food. Already laid out on the kitchen counter next to the stove I had stretched out large sheets of newspaper, black and white only, no color, ready to receive the delicate morsels as they were whisked from the hot oil with my new Asian bamboo and woven wire utensil. There, stretched out in one layer they would drain and receive a quick dusting of a medium grind sea salt, tossed by a hand movement like feeding a bunch of chickens in the barnyard. This gives the illusion of great confidence like the chef really knows what he is doing. The Asian equivalent of a flambé. Very important!

A new black lacquer serving platter sat nearby, awaiting the arrival of little crunchy critters, turned the color of little cooked lobsters. Yum!

With the oil at the perfect temperature I reached into the freezer, grabbed the plastic milk jug, and removed the cap. Ungi was really impressed, I could tell, with my culinary skills. I inverted the jug and quickly dumped all the frozen grasshoppers into the hot oil. We stood back a bit because there was a little snapping and popping as the hot oil reacted to the bit of moisture in the container. A second later, there was an explosion—not of fire, or hot bubbling oil—but of grasshoppers! Hundreds of grasshoppers as they came back to life and jumped everywhere—all over us, our hair, our clothing, the floor, the counter, the sink, the dining room, the couch, and everywhere else in the house a grasshopper could possibly jump to.

I remembered what the wise old man had told me.

You might say this was my culinary fall from grace.

But I *still* see Ungi from time to time, and I *still* have trouble with her accent. . . . but we still laugh, and still smile, about a most memorable evening together.

Benny and the Jets

BENNY WAS MY FATHER-IN-LAW, AND HE WAS A GOOD MAN. THE family referred to him in Polish as the Bahartek, or big shot. It was complimentary or jokingly used as a sign of respect. When the song "Benny and the Jets" came out by Elton John, we used it to identify ourselves, as the 'Jets'. Benny knew everyone, and vice versa. If he didn't have your name or if he didn't remember it, he just called you 'Chief'. That fit everyone except the women, who he didn't seem to forget as easily. If it was a waiter, he would call him Chief, until he learned otherwise, "like Hey Chief, how about some water, heh heh." That was another characteristic of his, "heh heh".

He was a jack of all trades, and ready to help wherever he could. He drove a big old Cadillac that I had given him instead of swapping it in as a trade. The trunk was huge, and he kept it full of tools, looking for chores, and his help was always well received. He was fascinated by how things worked. I remember him calling me over to him, "Allan, Allan, how the hell did those Egyptians ever build the Great Pyramids?" He obviously had already given it a great deal of thought, but just couldn't figure it. I offered my suggestion that "perhaps people were smarter then" and he rolled it around in his brain and said, "Allan, heh maybe, smarter then heh heh."

We got along very well. I remember him and his character, and his birthday, February 2nd, one day before mine. Maybe that had something to do with how we got along.

One night, Sue and I got a phone call from Stacia, Sue's mother, who was in a panic and wondering what to do. Benny had awoken with terrible pain in his gut and it was getting worse. Fortunately, we lived nearby and zoomed down to their cottage. I thought it might have been his appendix, but whatever it was we had to to get him safely to the hospital, and fast. Benny didn't want to go. He wanted to wait 'til morning and see how he felt. And everyone knew the ER and an ambulance were outrageously expensive, especially Benny. He lost that argument, and the next, which was for me to drive him to the ER myself. We just overruled him and his pocketbook. I was selected, for some reason, to be the family member to ride with the EMTs to the ER. Maybe because we had the Great Pyramid thing to figure out, or other things . . . I don't know.

It was a short ride, and the ER staff quickly ruled out a bunch of things and invented a few others for which they tested. The real culprit turned out to be a severely infected gall bladder. It had to come out. Now. It could do him in if not taken care of immediately. We got good advice, and a good surgeon, and the surgery went well according to all concerned. But for some reason Benny didn't just spring back. He was hospitalized for more than a month and still had all the tubes connected so they could feed him and keep him going. But he was not fully conscious. They did all they could for him but finally had to move him to a special care facility just over the border in Connecticut. But instead of showing improvement, he was slowly slipping away. The family visited him often, but we could see he was wasting away.

One day Sue and I, and Sue's sister, Lisa, went for a visit. We had to do something. We three were ready to see some action. We asked if we could put him in a wheelchair and push him around, but they said they had trouble lifting him to a chair. I volunteered to show them how it was done easily and safely—which I had learned while working at a hospital all through college. At that point we had him up, fastened in and ready for a stroll, so they couldn't say no.

Off we went, up and down the corridors. All of them. The staff watched us for a while and then kind of forgot about us. Benny still hadn't moved a muscle. The medical building was just one level and there were no steep inclines. We took advantage of their lack of oversight and pushed Benny outside. I ran to my car, brought it around and we somehow got Benny into the back seat with Lisa. The wheelchair stayed behind. We felt like Bonnie and Clyde, or kidnappers, and took off down the street, thinking this was just the kind of thing Benny needed—a nice ride. But it didn't bring him back to consciousness. At first, we only intended to take him for a quick ride, get him out, and stimulate him, but we got carried away and brought him to my house where we made him as comfortable as we knew how. At some point the medical facility must have discovered the empty wheelchair outside and called the police. The relatives started to get calls and they called us. The police were involved but hadn't pinned us down yet, but we realized it was just a matter of time, so we had better do something that would keep us out of jail. We could see the headlines: "Jets arrested for kidnapping Benny the Bahartek of Misquamicut Beach."

We called the medical facility and assured them we were on our way back, but Benny was resting at the moment, and when he woke up we would bring him right back. That bought us some more time. It seemed that they didn't want any negative news to fall on them like "Medical Facility loses patient" so they agreed and called off the manhunt for us and Benny. Benny slept like a log and we all slept soundly after the excitement of the day.

But, early in the morning we heard noises coming from the bedroom. Benny was trying to get up. He was thrashing in the bed and yelled my name when he saw me. "Allan, Allan, what's goin' on?"

We couldn't believe it. Benny was back! It must have been all the activity, the familiar surroundings, the cooking smells, and the sounds of the family jabbering away like they always did. It had all brought him back. That and the lack of sedation meds he was probably on. He got out of his sick bed and joined us at the breakfast table, acting like the Bahartek of Misquamicut, which he continued to be for 13 more years. Heh Heh!

Fresh Fish

JUST THE GENTLE SLAP, SLAP, SLAP—LITTLE RIPPLES—THE SOUND of water as it caught the bottom of our Sears and Roebuck aluminum 12-foot skiff. It was Buzz's boat. His family's. Lucky to have use of it, we kids. Practical, lightweight, quick enough with a small engine— better than anything else we had, and particularly well-suited to our task at hand. We sat anchored, as we had so many mornings, in the current, under where Sprague bridge used to be. That one is gone now but a new one took its place. The last one on Narrow River, before you came out to the ocean near the Dunes Club. It was peaceful, and would be, at least for a little while longer until the sun would paint the sky and finally emerge from below the sea, to above the horizon. Neither on land nor sea was there any traffic or noise this early. The air would soon be changing, still and foggy, warm and close, to that fresh coolness that signals the approaching dawn.

A streetlight on the bridge gave just enough light to see what we were doing . . . just enough to rummage through the little cardboard box inside of which was a little moist seaweed and half a dozen pulsing, pinching, squirming clam worms that we had irreverently woken up.

Our task was fishing. And just a few feet below us was a wonder world of creatures, waiting for breakfast. It was only about a 20-minute ride down the river to this favorite fishing spot. When our anchor was set, it was who gets fishing first, and who catches the first fish. It wasn't just the fish who were waiting for breakfast. . .

There were usually flounder, or "flat fish" as we called them, and sometimes black fish, who patrolled the river bottom. They both loved clam worms. Our anticipation was high, never knowing, except in our imaginative minds, what was happening below. . . and that's why they call it fishing, not "catching." But fortunately, we were often lucky.

And our reward? A hearty breakfast. As mentioned, our boat was particularly well suited to the task. At the very center, between us, on the floor of our aluminum boat, we set up a Sterno stove. Our lively, flapping fish were quickly cleaned, just moments after reaching the surface, and introduced to a waiting fry pan, sizzling with brown bubbling butter and a touch of salt. This was fresh fish. We split our time between catching and eating, and as each fish was shared between us, we would proclaim that this one was the best one we had ever tasted. And it was all you could eat, if you could catch 'em.

Sometimes, with early daylight, someone out on an early walk would notice us, as they peered down from the bridge, and sometimes they asked what we were doing down there. "Fishin'" one of us would say with a touch of music. Perhaps we should have said "Livin'" but certainly could have said "just making memories to last forever."

Photo: Carrie Capizzano

Allan Redfern was born and raised in Rhode Island but did not let the fact that he lives in the smallest state in the union deter him from being a world traveler. A teacher, an entrepeneur, a jack-of-all-trades, he finds adventure wherever he goes and is able to discover friends in the most faraway places.

Made in the USA
Middletown, DE
08 April 2021

37223267R00087